Visual Journalism

Journalism: Reflections on Practice

Series Editors: **Sarah Niblock**, Professor of Journalism and Head of Social Sciences, Media and Communications, Brunel University London, UK; **Rosalind Coward**, Professor of Journalism, University of Roehampton, UK

This series of titles seeks to provide students, academics and journalists with a unique practical and critical guide to key areas of contemporary journalistic practice in the digital age, interrogating the shifting contexts and practices in journalism, and demonstrating how real-world journalists navigate and accommodate everyday demands, challenges and opportunities in this dynamic industry.

Published titles:

Rosalind Coward
SPEAKING PERSONALLY

Murray Dick
SEARCH: THEORY AND PRACTICE IN ONLINE JOURNALISM

David Machin and Lydia Polzer
VISUAL JOURNALISM

James Rodgers
REPORTING CONFLICT

For more information on titles in the series, please visit www.palgrave.com/series/journalism/JRP/

Journalism: Reflections on Practice
Series Standing Order ISBN: 978–0–230–58080–0

If you would like to receive future titles in this series as they are published, you can make use of our standing order facility. To place a standing order please contact your bookseller or, in case of difficulty, write to us at the address below with your name and address and the name of the series. Please state with which title you wish to begin your standing order.

Customer Services Department, Macmillan Distribution Ltd, Houndmills, Basingstoke, Hampshire, RG21 6XS, UK

Visual Journalism

By
David Machin
and
Lydia Polzer

 palgrave

First published 2015 by
PALGRAVE

Palgrave in the UK is an imprint of Macmillan Publishers Limited, registered in England, company number 785998, of 4 Crinan Street, London N1 9XW.

Palgrave Macmillan in the US is a division of St Martin's Press LLC, 175 Fifth Avenue, New York, NY 10010.

Palgrave is a global imprint of the above companies and is represented throughout the world.

Palgrave® and Macmillan® are registered trademarks in the United States, the United Kingdom, Europe and other countries.

ISBN 978–0–230–36021–1

This book is printed on paper suitable for recycling and made from fully managed and sustained forest sources. Logging, pulping and manufacturing processes are expected to conform to the environmental regulations of the country of origin.

A catalogue record for this book is available from the British Library.

A catalog record for this book is available from the Library of Congress.

Typeset by MPS Limited, Chennai, India.

Printed in China

Contents

List of Figures

Acknowledgements

Many accomplished visual journalists agreed to being interviewed for this book. We would like to thank them for contributing their time and expertise: Lee Bearton (*Evening Standard*), Luka Boskovic (graphicriver), Nik Callan (eyecatchingdesign), Adis Cengic (graphicriver), Andy Cowles (IPC), Carrie Cousins, Julien Cousins (BBC), Michael Crozier (Crozier Associates), Kevin Curtis (BBC), Peter Day (BBC), Javier Errea, Shehani Fernando (formerly *The Guardian*), Elizabeth Galbraith (BBC *GoodFood*), Jonathan Goldberg, Michael Graae, Barry McIlheney (Periodical Publishers Association), Andrew Jackson (BBC GoodFood), David Levene, Alick Mighall (miggle.co.uk), Mel Nichols (formerly Haymarket Publishing), Ally Palmer (PalmerWatson), David Parry (PA), Matt Phare (Shortlist), Mark Porter (Mark Porter Associates), Louis Quail, Ron Reason, Alice Salfield (BBC), Marten Sealby (Ink Publishing), Alan Sparrow (Metro), Tom Stoddart, Adam Woodgate (Immediate Media Co).

The authors and publishers would like to thank the following copyright holders for permission to reproduce images in the text:

The Independent for *The Independent* front cover, Wednesday 3 June 1992 (Figure I.2);
Caspar Opitz at *Dagens Nyheter* for the *Dagens Nyheter* front cover, Wednesday 3 July 2013 (Figure I.3);
Getty Images and Tom Stoddart for Figures 1.1 and 1.2;
Kerry Black at *The Scotsman* and Michael Graae for *The Scotsman* inset, 25 February 2011 (Figure 1.3);
Michael Graae for Figure 1.4;
Louis Quail for Figures 1.5 and 1.6;
Jonathan Goldberg for Figures 1.7 and 1.8;
David Levene for Figures 1.9 and 1.10;
Elizabeth Galbraith and Andrew Jackson at BBC *GoodFood* for Figures 2.1, 2.2 (draft *GoodFood* front covers, January 2012), 2.3 (*GoodFood* front cover, January 2012) and 2.4 (*Olive* front cover, Issue 9);
Simon Johnsen for Figure 2.5;

Jocelyn Bowerman at Eye to Eye Media Ltd and *delicious* magazine for the *delicious* front cover, February 2014 (Figure 2.6);

Juliet Roberts at *Gardens Illustrated* for the *Gardens Illustrated* front cover, May 2014 (Figure 2.7);

Libération for the *Libération* front cover, 26 January 2014 (Figure 2.8), and Figures 2.9 and 2.10;

The *Evening Standard* for the *Evening Standard* front covers 15 October 2008 and 5 April 2013 (Figure 3.2);

Martin Buhagiar at *Harrow Times* for Figures 3.3 and 3.4;

Aamulehti for Figure 3.5;

Ron Reason and *Capital Ideas* for Figures 3.6, 3.7, 3.8, 3.9, 3.10 and 3.11;

David Harris, *Car and Accessory Trader (CAT)* magazine and Haymarket Media Group for Figures 4.7, 4.8 and 4.9.

Introduction: Visual Design as Systematic Communication

Journalism has received extensive scholarly study over the past three decades. This has tended to focus on national newspapers, on how and why they represent the world and events in the way that they do, and more recently on the falling circulations of these titles. But vast areas of journalistic work have actually been conspicuously absent from such studies. One of these neglected areas is the visual aspect of journalism. Yet the visual elements of media, the way in which they are employed, arranged and designed, be it in newspapers, magazines, on webpages, tablets and smart-phones or in television, contributes significantly to the message conveyed. Throughout this book, by examining the underlying principles of this visual work, along with its changing nature, we aim to demonstrate its central importance. This visual work is not mere dressing or appearance, but fuses with the very meaning of what is on the page or screen. And in contemporary print, digital and television journalism, it is now often the case that the product is built from a visual basis in the first place. In other words, content is collected and shaped to fit a newspaper or webpage that has a clearly formed visual identity.

While photojournalism has been taken more seriously, other visual aspects of news and journalism have tended to be sidelined as mere packaging. We argue throughout this book that the meaning of the written or spoken part of journalism, across different media, is communicated simultaneously by how it is presented visually. Rather, in fact, we would say how it is *realised* visually. We prefer this term here as we want to move away from the idea that the visual is independent from language and 'information'. Visuals do not simply supplement, or package, news, editorials or features, but form part of the ideas about the world, concepts and attitudes that are communicated. It is useful, we suggest, to acknowledge that news and journalism have always been intricately bound into ideas about what constitutes knowledge in a given society. Then conclusions can be made about what forms its communication might take and what kinds of sources can claim to provide this. In this book we track how these ideas have changed over time and now appear communicated with greater sensitivity and complexity in visual forms. Of course, new technologies have made this possible. But the way we communicate has itself changed. We may live in a more visual culture, but in addition to that the role of the visual and its relationship with language is certainly undergoing a far-reaching transformation.

News and journalistic work has always been produced for specific markets. Designers work on the layout of newspapers so that their content best speaks to a particular target group; a magazine designer must make the right visual and compositional choices to communicate the ideas, mood and identity of the title; a set designer must ensure that the look of a news studio is appropriate for the brand of the news programme and the attitude and mood it seeks to present to viewers. These visuals are not simply mere style or 'presentation' but form part of the way in which news creates meaning and also about the social relations they set up with readers, users and viewers. For example, a designer might ask: should a newspaper have lots of white space on the page to suggest lightness as opposed to filling all available space with condensed text? According to one newspaper designer whose work we look at in detail in this book, such choices change the meaning of the content itself, but also the meaning of the very medium itself and how it is perceived. He pointed out that formerly in design it was important for newspapers to present themselves as formal, important, authoritative and as containing all the information needed by a person who considered themselves as 'informed'. Here condensed text and crowded pages were necessary to signify this, even if in fact many of the items would go unread. Spreading text and contents out so that the page contains extensive amounts of white space is part of a shift in the market that now experiences the former authoritative newspaper as pompous, dull and conservative. This new lighter newspaper suggests something that is a distraction during a commute to work and speaks to someone who feels they should be communicated with as a shrewd thinking person rather than as a uninformed citizen. The information may be the same, but the visuals give it a different meaning and orient it towards different reader requirements and experiences. Design is not simply packaging or dressing but is part of the way the meaning of the contents is communicated.

In Figure I.1 we see a mock up design for a page by a professional magazine designer who freelances across many international titles. There is not yet any actual content on this page. Designers use a piece of Latin text called 'Lorem Ipsum' to mimic the look of real copy when creating mock ups, so they don't need the finished article to start laying out the

Figure I.1 Mock up for magazine design

page. And yet the visual choices made in this case already communicate clear ideas and attitudes. They set up a kind of social relationship between the title and the reader.

We can see in Figure I.1 that the designer has not yet decided on which of the 'cog' or 'bolt' type insets to use. But the choices in font, in visual elements, such as the cog and the computer keyboard shapes, along with the page structure and borders, communicate something of the ideas and attitudes the text might carry. The designer said that this design was for a magazine oriented towards a male market. The page uses three columns of main text to avoid a sense of dense reading. Design features, such as the very modern and slightly feminine font, the extensive use of space, along with a measured use of colour, speak to a more upmarket, younger, professional male. He might consider himself – in the language of marketing – more of a 'critical thinker', 'open minded' and 'style aware' (even if they may not necessarily be any of these things). The language style of the writing must of course speak to this target audience, too. And the advertisers buying ad space in this magazine will also be those who are aiming at that particular audience. Design and content together shape how the publication is perceived and received by the reader.

Visual design in journalism is an integral part of how meaning emerges from the content of news stories, with the people and events they cover. A reader will understand the news events carried by news outlets in a way that is fused with their visual appearance. In scholarly work there has been some attention to this in terms of the role of the photograph, but rarely in terms of more detailed visual choices such as page layout and the subtleties of a television set design.

What the designer of the page in Figure I.1 also stressed in her account of this magazine design was the range of issues relating to advertising, costs, staffing and technology that lay behind the path to producing the end product. To understand the visual choices we find in our newspapers, websites and other news outlets we must also understand the processes that lie behind the work of designers. In this book we analyse the work of these practitioners across a range of areas with the aim of pointing to basic and underlying principles of design. We also try to understand how designs respond to market needs and technological limitations as much as simply creating great aesthetics. Different chapters accomplish this in different ways. Some engage with scholarly research to look at how the visual journalists themselves view their job in the light of some of the criticisms raised. Other chapters explore how scholarly and theoretical models can work alongside the principles used across visual communication in journalism. But all the chapters seek to reveal underlying principles of design that will remain even as new platforms arrive. At the same time they provide insights into the way visual designers work and the changing environment in which they find themselves.

Running across the subject matter covered in this book is a common theme: the importance of the brand in the massively competitive multi-platform environment. We look at the huge amount of detailed, focused and highly skilled activity that lies behind the shaping of magazine content in order to address different markets and to create strong brand identities. We examine redesigned newspapers and how they use looks to chase specific advertiser-friendly target groups. Websites too get similar overhauls as sites compete to be news aggregators. We investigate how the presentation of television news is evolving as audiences have diminished, become more fragmented and perhaps most importantly as the role of news in society has changed. It can no longer represent itself as institutional, self-important, formal and grave. Again, importantly, this is not simply about a transformation of the packaging of news but a change in what news in itself means. In fact, one common thread across news design is the demasculinisation of news and the stripping away of authoritarian notions of old. The latest successful designs strive for a revamped relationship with readers and viewers, although in television there appears to be less certainty as to how this should be done.

Visual communication and digital media

Rapid changes are taking place in visual journalism with the shift to online, multi-media and multi-platform publishing. Magazines and newspapers are operating as websites and accessible on mobile phones with the possibilities for video content and interactivity. But while it might appear to the outside observer that the publishing industry is now the brave new world of digital journalism, the impression from inside the industry at the time of writing is one where traditional print production processes are still very much in place and where core visual design skills remain centrally important. There are many pioneers embracing new digital platforms and experimenting with their use. But many of the practitioners interviewed complain of a lack of financial support for digital content both from within the publishing industry as well as from advertisers. And it is clear that working practices are far from consistent and certainly not being shared across the industry.

Interviewees often remark on the promotional bluster that accompanies the announcement in the trade press of the latest versions of software and gadgets, which often are soon shown to be as unworkable as their predecessors.

There are those who firmly believe that the days of print journalism are numbered and that news and magazine delivery is about to become online only. While it is difficult to project just what might happen, the evidence at this time does not seem to corroborate this view. And certainly this appears to be a highly Anglo/Euro-American viewpoint as print titles and circulations continue to expand in many other parts of the world (Franklin, 2010).

In the interviews that we carried out for this book it became clear that there are huge competitive pressures among producers of journalistic content to embrace digital platforms. But in many cases the actual role of these platforms is not so clear, and these are consequently poorly supported by publishers. From the point of view of analysing visual design and communication in journalism these new online and mobile designs are nevertheless important. On the one hand, clearly many of the same basic principles of design apply. In our own experience of training journalists this can become overlooked when faced by the thirst to be using the latest technology, to be seen to be up-to-date. But, on the other hand, these new outlets are exciting as they bring a new dimension of interactivity into the reading experience. They influence the look of traditional print products as designers must create brand consistency across platforms. Also digital forms become the standard for indicating the latest in design. Increasingly designers must communicate with generations of readers who have grown up in the matured internet environment and who have no established culture of visiting the newsstand.

For many readers of this book it will be hard to imagine how important news-kiosks were as part of the daily routines of commuters, for example, even in the 1990s. But in both cases the role of the visual journalist remains the same. They must communicate ideas, attitudes and values using the right kinds of visual resources but in a context where this may be constrained by the specifics of technology, production processes and finances.

While we seek to identify what are, at the time of writing, new trends, processes and work practices in visual journalism, in the first place we want to provide a new theoretically informed account of some of the basic principles of the design and presentation of news. Chapters offer tools for analysing and building designs that are fundamental and enduring. In the first chapter, for example, we look at how the work of photojournalists has changed in recent times. We present a variety of different types of photographs produced for different markets. But we also reflect on the nature of photojournalism, what it is, some key patterns in its products and the role it plays in news and features. These observations are valuable for understanding the use and role of photographs and images across media, including digital media and television news. In the following chapters we cover magazine and newspaper design, first in print form and then in digital form. Of course, presently it can be the case that designers have to be mindful of designing for a title that will be multi-platform. But we do not want the basic processes of good design, of the precision with which visual designers communicate, to become obscured by this. Rather we focus on some of the commonalities between online and print design.

Design and globalisation

In journalism studies there has been an interest in a model of journalism that to a large extent has its origins in the UK and US (Chalaby, 1996) and that has been exported around the planet. Interest lies in how the practices associated with journalism have become adjusted and transformed through local culture and politics (Herbert, 2001; de Beer and Merrill, 2004) and broadly what the characteristics of journalism around the world are. Visual journalism here too is of relevance. Throughout this book we demonstrate that news, or a magazine feature, can have very different meaning depending on how it is realised visually. So to investigate the global spread and adaptation of a western invention called 'journalism' it is helpful to consider the visual forms that can themselves be globally adapted and modified in different settings. Many of the fundamental principles of design that we consider in this book, as we show, have in fact become basic resources internationally.

In fact, visual design is one area where the processes associated with globalisation have received little attention. One of the present authors has carried out research into the way that international magazine titles such as *Cosmopolitan* are modified both in terms of content, but also in terms of design (Machin and Van Leeuwen, 2007). Important among the findings of this research was how local magazine producers around the world were attempting to reproduce the look of international magazine titles. For example, interviews with the editor and designer of a Vietnamese magazine in 2003 pointed to the way that the increasing presence and availability of international titles had changed reader expectations of the look of magazines. This meant more attention to how design features such as font, colour, images and composition were used. Later versions of the magazine demonstrated this shift compared to earlier versions, which appeared, even in the view of the editors, as amateurish. The principles being increasingly followed are the same as those we explore in Chapter 2 of this book.

The same author was later involved in research on the changes in the design and language style of the Chinese magazine *Rayli* (Chen and Machin, 2013, 2014). Interviews carried out with the editor and designer revealed a gradual adoption of western styles of design in terms of the use of fonts, colours, image and composition. This change can be seen by comparing older and more recent page layouts. In older versions of the magazine the use of colour coordination is rather crude as compared to editions of the magazine from around 2011 onwards. In the old version fonts are only used to create hierarchy whereas in newer copies they are also used to create links across the design along with colour. Images are now also used as part of the design rather than more literally. In the case of *Rayli* designers spoke also of Japanese influences on the look of the magazine. But the systematic attention to how design features were used was directly influenced by international magazines such as *Cosmopolitan*, *Marie Claire* and *Men's Health*. And it is this level of design that is of interest to us in this book. While we cover all the different kinds of visual media, it is the core aspect of design, of knowing how to use basic tools systematically, that interests us. In the magazine in Figure I.1 the basic level of design is the way that typeface speaks to a male reader in a manner that communicates that he is more modern and thoughtful. *Rayli* magazine uses lighter, more modern typefaces to communicate a much softer, innocent kind of feminine identity. It is the particular theory of visual communication that we draw on in this book that provides a particularly useful way to characterise this deeper level of design.

What is also clear is that visual designers increasingly operate in an international environment. Michael Crozier, whose newspaper redesigns we focus on in a later chapter, has redesigned newspapers around the world. We also interview Javier Errea, who was one of the designers on the international award-winning Swedish newspaper *Dagens Nyheter*, but also a range of other titles across Europe and South America. Chicago-based Ron Reason has designed titles in India, New Zealand, North America and Europe. Each designer mentioned principles of design and spoke of its purpose and how both are common across national markets. Some of the photojournalists we spoke to told us that the production of editorial and creative images must now be understood in terms of a global market as photographs are most commonly sold by globally operating photo archives such as Getty Images (Hansen and Machin, 2008). The news set designers we interviewed had produced sets for news in Europe, Asia and North and South America. Research is needed beyond the scope of this book to consider the exact nature and importance of these trends. Of course, a news programme in Hong Kong may have a set produced by the same designer as a set in Italy. They may take all their images from the same global image archive. But the nature of the contents may be fundamentally different.

Reflective journalism

This book should also be seen in the light of a newer emphasis on reflective journalistic practice where there is a two-way process of academics and journalists interacting to think both critically and productively about the nature of journalism (Niblock, 2012). This trend has been motivated by a number of factors, which include more former practitioners now working in universities, which are themselves called upon to produce their own research. Also academic researchers have taken a renewed interest in the news production process, driven through a desire to understand this in its rapidly changing market. Across academic study of journalism this attention is often driven by a concern for the nature of democracy where it is assumed that the role of the journalist in maintaining an informed citizenship appears to be on the wane. Journalism studies acknowledge the need to bring together the knowledge and practices of journalists with academic theories and research where the former gains critical insights and the latter can develop more grounded accounts of journalism and its products. But there has been little work specifically on the analysis of visual design in journalism, let alone its practices and production processes.

In this book we allow experienced visual journalists to reflect on their work, to explain how and why it is done to provide a valuable resource for students and trainees. We interviewed 75 professionals working across design and photography. This involved a combination of face-to-face interviews where we discussed examples of their work often over several sessions, emails, telephone calls and Skype. Some were done in production settings such as in the case of magazine design especially, although most of the people we interviewed worked freelance. The site for these meetings was often the cafés where they, and many of their colleagues, would regularly be found working on their laptops. In each case rather than a single, more structured interview, we entered into dialogue with the journalists. In the first place we would approach them with examples of their work. We would ask basic questions about how the work was commissioned or decided upon, and the processes of its realisation. This would be followed by further thought and returning to the journalist with more specific questions, about how particular visual elements worked for them. Here one issue we found was that much design knowledge remains tacit. These people are skillful masters of delicate, careful and precise manipulation of the communicative resources of visual design. But they tend to report on these in terms of adjectives, like 'relaxing' or 'forceful'. When a newspaper designer says, 'we now have a whole new way of using images', it is hard to get them to pinpoint exactly what this means, even though on the page it is fully clear that such a transformation has taken place.

We also seek to critically engage with this work by taking this opportunity to produce more systematic critical and analytical observations on areas of visual communication in journalism that have yet to receive attention by scholars. And even in photojournalism theory it has tended to be treated in isolation from the actual practical concerns of what photojournalists think they are doing and what the organisations they work for actually require from them.

Entrepreneurial journalism

Scholars have also pointed to a newer issue for journalists, something that is only just beginning to be addressed on the curricula of more forward-thinking journalism training centres and crucial for the way that most of our interviewees operate. This regards the need for them to possess entrepreneurial skills (Baines and Kennedy, 2010). Journalists increasingly work as freelancers and need to promote their own work. One of the authors works in editorial and visual design in the magazine industry where there has, over the past ten years, been a switch away from full-time staff to employing freelancers, temps and interns. On the titles where she works it is possible that designers who have been involved in the production of more than one edition will be considered the authority as regards the brand identity of the title. Among the visual journalists we interviewed for this book, across photojournalism, newspapers, magazines, online and television there was a clear sense of a move away from permanent positions. Most interviewees worked alone, as freelancers, or for a small and sometimes highly successful, independent design company. There is an increasing awareness that training needs to incorporate a sense of how the market works. As we present the work of each of the visual journalists we will be giving insights into how the industry is now structured and also into how work is found by some of the visual journalists.

All of the photographers and designers we interviewed for this book possessed a powerful sense of the market for their work and also had clearly developed professional insights into how branding is fostered and maintained. The co-author of the present book, who also works as a designer, was familiar with using core design skills to provide quick design solutions for often very carefully described target groups. Designers we spoke with who worked for some of the older, bigger publishers, such as the BBC, spoke of knowing and understanding their readership intuitively. In contrast the freelancer may work on many designs at once, with little turnaround time and going on basic market information.

This attention to niche markets and branding has been said to ask new questions of the professional identities of journalists (Lowrey and Anderson, 2005; García, 2008). Formerly at the heart of this professional identity has been the commitment to neutrality and fairness. But how do these new skills requirements and the demands of the new working environment influence this? One of the biggest changes being experienced by the magazine industry at the time of writing was the shift to online and other portable formats – even if in fact digital copies of magazines – usually in PDF form and accessible online through a browser – still only accounted for 1% of total sales in 2011 (*Press Gazette*, August 2011). Loraine Davies of the Periodical Training Council in the UK told us that one big change in the magazine industry had been in terms of recruitment, where even the bigger publishers require staff to be multi-skilled and technologically literate – a staff designer may also be required to manage websites, create short clips for YouTube and engage with social media. One concern for the Council was that there was no clear direction for publishers as regards skills requirements as new cross-platform magazine formats were still searching for established business models.

A multimodal approach to visual communication

While this book gives insights into the practical side of working in visual design and communication in journalism it also seeks to contribute a theoretical understanding of design. To do this we describe and analyse visual design through an emerging tradition in visual communication theory called Multimodality. This provides a more predictive set of tools for breaking down and analysing the visual appearance of journalistic output. It furnishes us with a set of inventories that we can use to understand specific design decisions and with a set of resources for building our own designs. While practice-based books approach design through notions of experience, creativity and good ideas, the approach we use here is designed to be more predictive and closely document what takes place in design.

A magazine or webpage designer is harnessing very specific choices of visual resources in order to communicate specific and coherent messages. But if we asked a number of readers what impression they had of these designs, they might explain that one is 'lively', another is 'serious' and another 'romantic'. If we pressed them, they might make comments on specific details, saying perhaps that the colours used on the website were 'moody' or 'conservative'. So for the magazine in Figure I.1 they may say it is 'serious' but 'accessible', without really knowing or being able to put into words what leads them to that conclusion. The reader is not describing the actual composition itself but rather the effect of the choices of elements and arrangement. In this book we are interested precisely in the complete process that eventually leads to the finished products being perceived in various ways by their audiences. And to do this, we draw upon the analytical framework of Multimodality.

Processes of design are still discussed in terms of effect, adjectives and as aesthetic choices rather than by being able to refer to the concrete and specific choices of visual resources. What exactly is it that would constitute a 'romantic' as opposed to 'rational' typeface? How might photographs be best positioned on a page to make sure the viewer's attention is correctly directed? What kinds of features make a more dramatic news set? What Multimodality does is direct our attention to describing the specifics of these choices.

Multimodality has its origins in linguistics and specifically in the Social Semiotic approach to language of Michael Halliday (1978). This is a theory of language that emphasises the way that when we communicate we have an available set of choices, which are finite in number. This includes both the set of words that we have and grammar. A speaker can use these options in creative combinations, although patterns should be followed as these are required for communication, even though this may involve subverting these patterns for irony, perhaps.

The linguist can therefore document what these underlying choices are and examine how they are used in actual contexts. The same set of assumptions was later applied by analysts to look at visual communication (Hodge and Kress, 1988; Kress and Van Leeuwen, 1996, 2001; Machin, 2007). From this has sprung a set of tools that can allow us to look more precisely at the details of the choices made in any kind of image, design or visual composition. It allows us to progress from describing design decisions only in aesthetic terms. Crucially it brings the possibility of a more systematic and critical approach to visual communication.

Multimodality is therefore simply an approach that breaks down compositions into their most basic components and to lead to an understanding of how these work together. Where a designer will give aesthetic reasons for choices in a composition, a multimodal approach systematically describes the range of choices available and shows how they are used in context. It explains why an image might be placed in a frame or not, whether this should be a wider or slimmer frame, whether saturated or more dilute colours should be used, whether an angular or curved typeface is better in a particular case. We look at the options available to designers and how they can be described in terms of inventories of possibilities.

Multimodality has much in common with traditional approaches to semiotics, which explore how individual signs connote or symbolise. Using the semiotics of Barthes (1978), for example, we might observe that a set for a news programme has used particular designs of chairs and table to communicate comfort and therefore a less informative and more 'chatty' approach to the news items. It might also use muted pastel colours to point to a more relaxed mood.

The Multimodal approach, by contrast, is interested in the underlying available repertoire for things like colours and composition. It analyses how these signs work together in combination and the potential each sign has to create meaning when used in contexts. In a Multimodal approach we would first deal with colour, for example. Does the set use brighter or darker colours? Are they more saturated or diluted, more pure or impure; do we find a broad or narrow colour palette? A set that used a broader colour palette would suggest more fun and playfulness than one with a limited palette. A set with more dilute colours might suggest a more relaxed mood than one with richly saturated colours. A set with impure colours might suggest more difficult issues than one with pure colours. Finally, brightness can suggest openness, truth and optimism, whereas darkness can suggest greater gravity, concealment and bleakness. Immediately we see here that it is possible to break down the design into more of its detailed choices. We can then go on to look at surfaces, for example. Do they suggest hardness or softness, roughness or smoothness, roundedness or angularity? Again we can look at the meanings of these variables.

These inventories of meanings can help us to look at the precise kinds of ideas and attitudes that are being infused into a particular design. If it is a news bulletin, the design may indicate that it is a more relaxed after-noon set, with muted colours, bright optimism and softer gentle edges. An evening bulletin may have darker colours, a more limited palette and sharper edges for seriousness.

There are a few key terms that help to clarify the way that Multimodality understands design. We use the idea of 'resources' throughout the book. In the model of language from which Multimodality is developed, a com-municator creates meaning by selecting from the available resources in order to achieve their particular goal. In language this simply means that they will choose certain words and certain grammatical forms when they speak to convey their message. If a teacher wishes to tell students that they must hand in their essays in one week, they will use a grammatical form that suggests that it is something that they simply must do. It is an instruction, not an invitation. In this view of communication speakers are aware of these resources and how they can be deployed in order to best accomplish their communicative goal. In the same way we can think about the qualities of colour we just considered for the news set as resources. In this case the set designer has a particular communi-cative goal and is, on one level, aware of the resources that will allow them to best achieve this goal. Of course, how well the resources are understood, used and combined and even a clear perception of what the particular communicative goal is, will depend on the skill and experi-ence of the designer.

Another key term we use is 'meaning potential'. In the case of lan-guage the meaning created by the choice of a single word depends on how it is combined with other words. In this sense language should be seen as a set of resources that have meaning potentials. In the same way we should not think about visual design elements, such as the qualities of a font or a colour, as having fixed meaning but as having meaning potential. They will have established meanings and associa-tions, but these are only activated when used in combination with other elements. The designer or visual journalist here is a skillful user of semi-otic resources with a keen sense of how to use them in specific contexts.

And as times change, as indeed they are, the designer or visual journalist has the talent and know-how to find new ways to use these resources, to find new ways to combine them, and even to find some completely new ones. Readers too share in this sense of meaning potentials, which makes this type of communication between designers and their audiences possible in the first place, but they are simply not so skilled in their actual use. And in this book, while we look over magazine design, web design and television set design, while the technologies and the formats differ, what unites them are the basic design skills, the basic ability of visual journalists to harness visual semiotic resources to accomplish specific communicative goals.

How we should formulate these 'communicative goals' of visual designers is also important for using this book and for understanding our particular approach to design. When trainees talk about their own designs they often say something like 'it needs to catch the eye', or 'stand out'. But to the visual journalists who need to address specific niche markets with their designs this is a meaningless thing to say. All designs must rather 'speak' to their intended audience. They must communicate the right kinds of ideas and attitudes to them. In Figure I.1 above we can say that the magazine design communicates the right kinds of ideas and attitudes to a particular educated, professional male reader in order for them to feel that it addresses *them*. But what we mean by ideas and attitudes can be broken down into something a little more systematic and of practical use for the purposes of design analysis.

Halliday (1978), Kress and Van Leeuwen (2006) and Kress (2010) argue that for any semiotic system to be considered a system it must fulfil three roles or three basic communicative functions. So, for example, a colour or typeface must be able to fulfil these functions. Explaining what these three functions are and how these can be fulfilled is important for us to move away from the idea of 'catchiness' to one of 'appeal for a specific market'.

The first of these three communicative functions is the *ideational metafunction*. Here a semiotic mode must be able to communicate ideas 'outside' of itself. In the case of language, for example, the word 'freedom' can communicate complex and powerful ideas. In the case of visual communication a wide typeface can communicate the idea of strength and stability while a very slim typeface, in contrast, would suggest weakness. In other contexts a wide font can suggest heavy and cumbersome, and a light, slim one elegance and aspiration. So a designer wishing to communicate the idea of solidity or the idea of elegance may use these qualities of typeface. In later chapters we see such uses of typeface across magazines, newspapers and websites.

The second of the three communicative functions is the *interpersonal metafunction*. Here a semiotic system must be able to communicate attitudes. In language we can use different moods of address to tell people our relationship to our ideas. So we can tell someone through an imperative mood 'do that!', or use the interrogative mood and ask them 'could you do that?' Saturated colours can suggest more intense moods whereas more dilute colours can suggest more muted moods. The designer of a webpage may want to suggest intensity, emotional exuberance or fun. Or they may want to suggest ease, relaxation, restraint.

The third communicative function is the *textual metafunction*. This suggests that a semiotic system must have coherence among its parts, as in grammar in language. In the case of visual communication different-shaped fonts can be used to create salience or hierarchy on a page. The same can be done with colour.

The metafunctions are one starting point for the analysis of the communicative role each element in a design plays, and what goal the visual journalist is pursuing. It is not so much that design elements 'catch the eye' of a reader, but that, along with the content, the visual design must communicate the appropriate ideas and attitudes to the desired reader.

Changing and more sophisticated use of visual communication tools

In Multimodality studies (Kress and Van Leeuwen, 2001) there is an interest in the changing way that different kinds of semiotic resources have been used by designers. Here the idea is that it is not so much that we now live in a more visual culture, as many assume, but that the role formerly taken by language has increasingly been replaced by other modes of communication. In fact, the whole way that we communicate is changing. The previously segregated role of the different semiotic modes, of language and different visual elements such as colour, has changed. Formerly these modes were used more in isolation. So writing and images would be separate on a page. The writing would provide information and the image an illustration of the case. For example, in a schoolbook there would be a picture of an animal and then below information about its habitat and behaviour. In more contemporary schoolbooks, in contrast, a picture of the animal might lie in the centre of the page, with small snippets of texts and other images and diagrams being placed around it. And whereas formerly it may have been entirely the language that conveyed how we were to take the information in terms of mood and attitude, now this might be communicated by the colour and typeface that might indicate that learning is fun, or scientific. More recently utility bills, which formerly carried basic numerical information about levels of usage, money due and instructions, will use more rounded fonts and dilute colours to suggest more muted moods, and lots of white space to suggest 'room to breathe'. So these visual tools are used to represent ideas and attitudes about the bill and its payment.

In an interview with Michael Crozier, who has redesigned newspapers around the world, we were told how in the 1990s in particular newspaper design was transformed, as things like colour, font, images and composition became thought of in much more systematic ways. It was not just that newspapers began to become colour versions of their former selves, Crozier said, but that they needed to rethink how this resource could be harnessed to speak to readers. One of Crozier's award-winning and innovative redesigns in the 1990s involved the British broadsheet *The Independent*, seen in Figure I.2. Crozier spoke of the way that in this case the editor gave over the entire cover to the graphics team. Rather than conceiving of the cover in terms of columns of text, they began to think about the way that images, colour and fonts could help to communicate about issues. Entirely new graphic elements and shapes were introduced, completely reframing the look of newspapers. Crozier said that it was not just a matter of newspapers using more visual elements, of becoming colourful, but of rethinking how they communicated.

These design choices should not just be thought of as being based on fashion or aesthetic changes. Such choices serve to communicate kinds of values and ideas about what is depicted. A woman's lifestyle magazine might be designed with colours, typeface, composition and use of particular photographs that suggest a particular lifestyle and address a confident, independent female reader. These visual elements play an important role in systematically aligning the products that are advertised in the magazine with the advertisers' desired consumer group. A newspaper must use font and colour to communicate specific ideas, attitudes and identities. *The Independent* began to address the public as different kinds of readers and to reshape its attitude to news presentation, also through design. Through Multimodality we would seek to identify the specific visual semiotic choices that allow these attitudes and values, these 'effects', to be communicated.

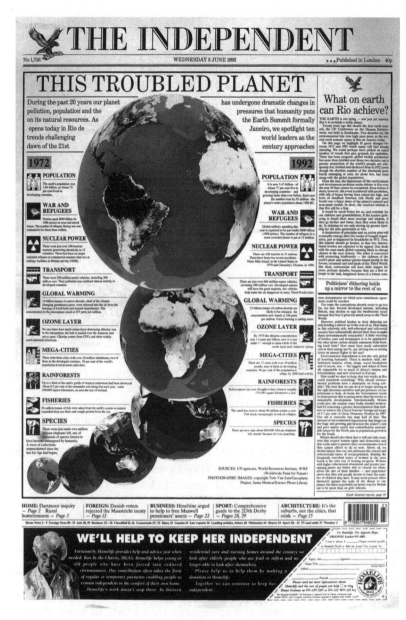

Figure I.2 *The Independent* (1992) with innovative cover design

Figure I.3   The award-winning Swedish newspaper *Dagens Nyheter*

It is important, however, to stress that Multimodality is the study of the communicative resources that we use in specific contexts. But we cannot understand exactly what these contexts are without engaging with producers. In Figure I.3 we see a cover of the design-award-winning newspaper, the Swedish *Dagens Nyheter*. This is a newspaper taking up innovation two decades after *The Independent* in Figure I.2. One of the design team, Javier Errea, told us that this design was partly to bring the newspaper back from a period where it had shifted more towards a tabloid look. Here the new design needed to combine font qualities to maintain a sense of 'informing' but also point to elegance and something less masculine. It was also influenced by the need to think about how it would be read on mobile devices. Images at the top and the configuration of story teasers appear as slabs familiar to tablet designs. This creates different kinds of design requirements than were necessary in the case of the innovative *Independent* in Figure I.2. Errea told us that the masthead deliberately uses a font that provides a mix of width, suggesting durability and slimness, hinting at subtlety. It also brings together angularity, such as in the sharp 'T', and rich curves as on the 'S' and 'R'. In terms of a multimodal analysis we would say that the angular and technical is combined with the curves of emotion. Errea drew attention to the unusual type of photograph used in this front cover, where the reader is allowed to see the scene from the viewpoint of one of the participants, as we look over their shoulder. In Multimodal terms here we would see a shift in the paper's relationship with the reader, involving them in the news rather than just providing information. It is unlikely such a Multimodal analysis would help a talented and greatly experienced designer such as Errea. But it can help us to more broadly and systematically think about how the resources of design can be deployed to achieve specific goals.

This opening chapter and the cases of design mentioned here set the tone for the chapters that follow. Each deals with fundamental design principles that we seek to identify and document. Aside from drawing on the aforementioned Multimodal theory, we rely also upon the accounts of the designers themselves. In each chapter we show how design principles are applied in each given media platform. It is these principles, after all, as our interviewees suggest, that underpin all good design work.

1 Photojournalism: Documenting and Symbolising Events

The news photograph has been associated with lofty ideals, such as providing visual evidence and bearing witness. It has also been criticised for its place in tabloid journalism, and in academic work has been held to be highly limited and even misleading. But as we show in this book the photograph has also become increasingly relevant as part of visual design. The news photograph, to an extent, has been rethought as a design feature, to lift a page, to communicate ideas and attitudes about the identity of the newspaper or magazine using it and of their readership. Javier Errea, designer of the award-winning Swedish newspaper *Dagens Nyheter*, spoke to us about the innovative ways that high-quality, visually striking images were used throughout this paper's design. Such photographs were no longer about 'bearing witness' as such but were part of a communicative strategy that suggests a more creative and thoughtful way of looking at the world. This then is not so much about what photographs depict, but about the ideas and attitudes the style of the photograph can get across. This is important for the new generation of readers. Ron Reason, a designer of many leading newspapers around the world, spoke of the more creative use of photojournalism alongside stock images and infographics. He explained how they are used more to symbolise the ideas behind a story rather than to document a particular moment.

We will be looking at photographs in relation to their placing within a page composition in more detail in later chapters. In this chapter we focus first on the modern photojournalist at work, and how they no longer merely record reality, nor document actual moments in time. They create more complex imagery symbolising broader ideas about events, which vary according to different kinds of news outlets. They are naturally aware of the change in the landscape of editorial photography. So photographers we spoke to talk about the challenge of taking more creative-looking images that must be in harmony with newspaper or magazine brands. While academic theories of the photograph tend to talk in terms of the representation of truth and reality, photojournalists tend to talk about the need to sell photographs, the demands of markets, picture editors and news cycles. Although, out of this process, some very compelling work still emerges.

We present the work of four photojournalists who operate at different levels: in a contracted position at one national newspaper, freelancing globally for supplements and international newspaper features, for local newspapers and producing news imagery for a stock-image library. We analyse the different types of images they generate for different markets, how they sell their work and how they understand the requirements of different newspapers.

Initially we briefly review the scholarly literature on photojournalism. This is highly useful for several reasons. First, the literature provides a range of ideas and concepts that can help us to think about how photographs communicate. This is important both in this chapter and in subsequent chapters where we look at the use of images in page designs, online and in television graphics. Second, there is need in bringing journalism theory and practice together. It will show how the accounts of the photojournalists we interviewed about their work tally with scholarly accounts. We prove, in fact, that to some extent the photojournalists tend to be mindful of the kinds of criticisms that academics have made of the news photograph. They may use a different vocabulary to express their thoughts about it. But it suggests that scholars may have misunderstood what photojournalism actually is. We end the chapter by connecting the newer trend of citizen-produced photojournalism to the discussion.

Theories of photojournalism

Academic discussions on the nature of the photograph, on what it does, on how it communicates provide a useful introduction to the work of photojournalists. This work seems to ask an awful lot of individual photographs that would not be asked of individual news texts. Photographs appear, at least on one level, to carry what has been called a 'burden of truth' (Newton, 1998). They are held up to a standard of bearing witness to reality. The basic criticism of photojournalism has been that photographs are limited. So the photojournalist who has been seen to operate, in the liberal perspective on news, as the eyes of the public, also stands accused of consistently failing in that task.

And yet they are the source of many iconic images of our times, such as Catherine Leroy's images of the American war in Vietnam or Jeff Widener's 'Tank Man' in Tiananmen Square. These are powerful images communicating eloquently about complex social and political issues and really contributing to humanity's understanding of news events, past and present.

But scholars have pointed out two problems with the news photograph. Firstly, photographs and video footage provide only selected moments from the flow of reality. Sontag (2004) sees photographs as 'reality interrupted', Berger (1980) as something seized from ongoing experience. In other words, photographs are representations that are isolated from the events that come before and afterwards. They are not therefore authentic representations of that process of events. Sontag (2004) points to the way that photographs tend to be used as they appear to encapsulate a series of complex events. The danger, she argues, is that news photojournalism has encouraged us to think about the world of events in terms of memorable moments rather than lengthy complex processes. And to some extent the fragmented nature of these compelling images also encourages us to accept a news world of unconnected, largely decontextualised events (Morley, 1992). Sontag (1973) argued that with news images anything can be separated or framed as adjacent to anything else. The world becomes 'a series of unrelated, free-standing particles' (p. 22).

Secondly, the processes that lie behind the taking of a photograph also pose a challenge to its eye-witness status. The selection of the shot itself, angle, proximity, exposure, cropping, later editing and then the editorial decision to choose this particular image over another, all become invisible due to the compelling nature of having the visual document in front of our eyes (Goldman and Beeker, 1985). Huxford (2004) points out that what is most worrying about all the conventions of photography is that they are unnoticed by the viewer. She notes it is easy to mistake proximity for association and an uneven, candid shot with frank and immediate reporting. An accused person comes across as evil simply because the picture of them frowning has been chosen over one with a neutral expression. Of course another thing we don't tend to see as viewers is the way images are placed on a page, how they are juxtaposed with headlines, page borders and other images.

Finally, and of central importance to the way photojournalists we interviewed work, is that photojournalists have to provide images that fit with established news frames. News frames are basic themes that have become established within news culture. They signal to a journalist that an event is newsworthy and how this event should be covered, who the key actors are and how they should be treated. It is thought within journalism that such frames are often necessary for the public to recognise an event as news, although to some extent they have become invisible to the practitioners themselves. These frames, therefore, are routinely used to structure how events are represented. For example, one news frame could be 'conflict/consensus'. A journalist seeking to structure a story about a student protest over cuts in education funding around this frame will tend to focus on violent or dramatic clashes between students and police, for example. The complexities of funding, privatisation or likely outcomes for the education system don't fit into that frame. In terms of images and video footage we will most likely see students destroying property and bloodied police officers. The narrative will speak of ring-leaders, respectable residents, damage costs and political statements promising to punish such lawlessness. The actual context that leads to the protests may therefore be largely ignored. Of course it is difficult to photograph abstract themes such as 'funding', 'privatisation' or 'education systems', and the symbols employed in the context of news frames might be the only vocabulary available to the photographer.

While academic work points to these limitations, this appears to be exactly how professional photographers work. They are aware of news frames, news flows, the need to capture the 'essence' of a story. It is these frames and structures against which they sell their work. But whether such processes prevent photographers from bearing witness is a different matter. In the field of social anthropology it has been common to think that it is not possible to objectively report on the social world of events. But many photojournalists do attempt to represent the world faithfully. But they do this as jobbing professionals with a sense of working for specific markets, all showing a keen sense of what kinds of images will suit the changing needs of specific publications that seek to address readers in new ways. It seems that we need a newer approach to the photograph that views it as part of communication, as a design resource that can work with other page elements including writing, rather than as an independent entity that in itself carries the burden of truth. In the Introduction we looked at the front page of *Dagens Nyheter*. The chosen cover image both seeks to literally 'bear witness' to an event, but also signals the ideas and attitudes held by the title and understood by its readers. Other page elements are deployed to the same end. This is an up-to-date, involved view on the world. For the designer here the photograph becomes part of the brand.

Photojournalism: Authenticity, symbolism and style

Tom Stoddart: Several decades of classic photojournalism

Tom Stoddart has been responsible for capturing some of the iconic moments of the past 30 years in captivating images. His style is widely recognised, often seen in emotionally taut, slightly haunting, black and white photographs. His pictures are licensed globally by Getty Images, appear across leading publications around the planet and have been part of highly successful exhibitions. These have included photographs of famines and various war zones. All tend towards striking and stark individual experiences of the people who inhabit these extreme environments.

Examples of Stoddart's work can be seen in Figures 1.1 and 1.2, taken during the conflict in Sarajevo in the 1990s. In the first we see a disturbing image of a hotel, as it might be typical to many cities, completely blown apart in this conflict. The second shows a woman walking defiantly in a street as snipers sit in the buildings above. These images are classic of the Stoddart style.

Figure 1.1   Sarajevo Holiday Inn, 1993
Source: Tom Stoddart, Getty Images

Figure 1.2   Woman defies snipers, Sarajevo, 1993
Source: Tom Stoddart, Getty Images

Stoddart has produced classic and memorable images across a range of conflicts and world events including the famine in Sudan – showing harrowing yet unsensational images of stick-thin people going about their business, burying their children and racing to a food drop; the earthquake in India – showing arms reaching out of rubble; the conflict in Iraq – where soldiers are shown wounded and in pain.

These images, in one sense, contain all the best features of photo-journalism. Such images may not inform about wider context, but they call upon us to think about ordinary worlds and lives, like our own, torn apart. Stoddart has said that such images are about seeing into the eyes of the people and grasping what they are thinking without them seeing you.

Stoddart has travelled to Sarajevo on several occasions, but spent three weeks there when the image in Figure 1.2 was taken. He had noticed how women not involved in actual combat held the family together and suffered for it. He had been struck by how brave and resilient the women were, and decided he would build a photo essay to document their everyday lives. He told us that he did this by observing them at the hospital where they worked as nurses or where wounded women could be found. Or he would just observe them in the streets. He heard stories of how the women joked about the fact they had to run everywhere to avoid sniper fire, saying this was a form of 'sniper-alley diet plan'. One woman he had been interviewing had been hit three times and used her X-rays as moulds to make candles. Others told how they fiercely avoided sex owing to the risk of creating more mouths to feed with no contraception available.

The image of the woman walking along the street turned out to be the lead image in this particular photo essay. Tom felt that this summed up what these women were about. And for twenty years this image has appeared in newspapers and magazines around the world. The woman in the picture walks down a street occupied by snipers, confident in her stance and in her decision to wear nice clothes and high heels. Women would normally avoid these kinds of clothes due to the need to run.

He said that on the one hand his intention was to document the lives of these women. But he also acknowledged that 'for a photo essay you need striking images'. In this case, he pointed out, it is all perfect: 'The way her hand is, the way her head is.' He said that such an image involves both luck and skill. The luck is that the image had the sandbags, the policeman, that she was dressed the way she was and walking in this fashion. He said that when he saw the woman coming along the street he backed away as he knew that the soldier was there guarding the building. And it is at that point, he noted, that the skill of a professional photographer comes in. They know what will make the image work, which spot to position themselves in and what angle is going to make the photograph stronger.

He said that good pictures should have 'about eight things going on in them that you can look at ... instead of one'. He said that if it had been an image just of the woman walking along, it would not have worked as there would have been fewer things to look at. In this case we also have the policeman, the gun, the cigarette in his hand. The fact his face cannot be seen keeps the focus on the woman. The contrast between the light flowery appearance of the woman's dress and the dark combat fatigues and gun of the soldier add to the tension in the image.

Stoddart also said that while sometimes good photographic moments can appear by chance a photographer comes to understand where good pictures will come from. For example, he said that he would sit in sniper alley, which many people had to cross, so a good image was likely to come about eventually. He said that he would also spend time in grave-yards photographing women visiting their husbands' graves.

We also asked to what extent these images were produced with a market in mind. Stoddart said that this was not a consideration. Although being a famous photojournalist known for a particular style, he tends to get commissioned for his own specific style of work. He did acknowledge that he would always have a strong sense of where images would likely be published. He would know that his photo essay of the woman of Sarajevo would be published by women's magazines looking to balance positive images of strong females against those of fashion and models. In fact he went back to Sarajevo twenty years later to photograph the same women, again knowing that this would generate interest, as publishers such as *Figaro* and *Marie Claire* would likely want to use them and even republish the original images alongside them for comparison.

In the same way Stoddart documented a week in the life of the British Prime Minister David Cameron. He went to Cameron's advisors after having heard on the news that Cameron was being criticised for not working hard enough. Stoddart told them he could create a photo essay to show just how much Cameron did in a week. At the same time he knew that *The Times* newspaper was running a series of photo essays on this topic where he could then place the images.

Images like those produced by Stoddart have been celebrated for the way they bring us close to the experiences of people living their lives during newsworthy events. As Stoddart says, he seeks to capture the spirit of what the experience is about for these people. These remarkable images give us a sense of access to a world otherwise inaccessible to us.

But to what extent do such images replace the complexity that lies behind them, as Sontag argues, through the need to produce memorable moments? Stoddart himself complained that such images are marketable and aestheticised, and become part of what is thought of as 'good documentary' rather than part of any political process.

Berger (1980) objected to how such images do not ask us to be critical but become part of the flow of the anticipated atrocities and violence in the world. The viewer then simply feels helpless given the constant stream of such events. Scholars such as Parry (2010) and Bouvier (2014) demonstrate that viewers are familiar with seeing images of war and disasters that emphasise their 'human toll' rather than the politics. This means that they will see a disproportionate number of images of women and children to tug the heartstrings of the Western viewer.

Notably Stoddart's images are simply not typical of those we now see in the mainstream press. He told us that his own position is unique. In view of his long career his images are often commissioned simply for their look and their connotations of artisticness, given that his work has frequently formed part of well-attended exhibitions. But it does not follow that newspapers will want to run them, and younger photojournalists, as we shall see, need to be much more market-oriented in terms of the work they produce. Stoddart spoke at length of the changing nature of the photojournalism industry where the increasing dominance of image archives such as Getty Images has led to a culture of using stylised photographs that are designed to sit well on the pages in the context of lifestyle marketing. But, we suggest, such changes are also related to wider changes in visual communication and reader/viewer expectations.

Freelance war and conflict photographers Louis Quail and Michael Graee

We met two other photojournalists who have – among other things – covered war. This is courageous, tenacious photography, often mainly carried out by freelancers who are prepared to push harder and act independent of employers who are less inclined to put employees in danger. But these photographers have a keen sense of the market for their images and of the need for images to also point to the identity of a title.

In this case the images we look at come from Libya. The British news media have themselves expressed regret about the lack of quality and simple errors of their coverage of this particular conflict including their visual representations of it. We need to say just a little about this to contextualise the photographs that were produced.

The BBC explained that there had been a too rapid acceptance of the definitions provided by official sources about the 'people's uprising' against Gaddafi. A range of outlets such as the *Economist* (Apr 1, 2011) then documented how the conflict was more of an elite struggle for control of the country's oil, with the NATO powers willing to back those prepared to make a deal with them (Bouvier, 2014; *The New York Times*, August 22, 2011). Moore (2011), writing in *The Telegraph*, spoke of the fudging of the reasons for the NATO powers to go and crush Gaddafi as part of an 'oil grab'. What was also clear, even before the conclusion of the war, were the difficulties that lay ahead for the formation of a stable government given the complexity of tribal and regional affiliations in the country that had come to the surface in the course of the conflict. These were largely absent from the news coverage. Bouvier (2014), carrying out a study of news photographs of the conflict, argues that the conflict was simplified through photographs of small groups of people waving flags or rag-tag groups of civilians carrying weapons amidst burnt-out vehicles. There were no images of the actual NATO attacks, or combat, only images of aircraft in hangars and in flight.

The two photojournalists we spoke to took photographs of the conflict that have appeared in the British national press. We look at their comments on how the images were produced and why. The first produced images in Libya during the conflict, the second a year on.

Michael Graae, a young photojournalist from New York, who had recently completed a BA in Photojournalism at the London College of Communication, decided to begin freelancing work in places like Libya during his studies. He researched some of the background to how the events had developed and also investigated points of entry to the country. He flew to Cairo and then drove 18 hours to Bengazi. He knew which areas to avoid as he had established that the BBC had tried to get in through the western border with journalists' visas but had been turned away and had equipment smashed up. He also read up on the Lockerbie bombing, and Gaddafi and his sons. He said that it was important to go in with a background understanding of the situation, not least because he needed to have an idea where he would need to go to generate some good images. Graae also said that to produce a proper photo essay on an area you need to spend at least two weeks there before you even start shooting.

Graae made some striking comments on which images tend to get chosen over those that do not, which help us to think a little more about why such images appear. He said that sometimes newspapers simply want photographs that sit well with their story. So the *Sun* ran stories on what it was like living in Bengazi. They focused on Gaddafi's former compound that had been looted. They took the angle that Gaddafi was simply an insane dictator living like a king. In fact one of the reasons behind the push to overthrow Gaddafi was that he had decided to redistribute the oil money into public services as reported by the *Economist* (2011). Graae had a picture of the shattered compound so the *Sun* used this, along with an inset of Gaddafi. This was also used by *The Scotsman*, as shown in Figure 1.3.

Graae once sought an explanation from a paper why out of a selection he had submitted a particular picture was used and was told that it was down to layout considerations. A picture editor may choose whichever picture sits better with other material on the page. Graae found that on his first trip there was more demand for 'destruction type' images, but that as time went on news attention shifted and interest turned to more 'humanitarian and recovery' images.

In the 'recovery' images we would find photographs of people carrying out more mundane activities amidst scene elements that indicated that there had formerly been conflict. And later there would also be the

Figure 1.3   Photograph by Michael Graae, seen with inset in *The Scotsman*, February 25, 2011

chance for the 'one year on' images, as in the photograph of the young girl in Figure 1.4, with the flag captioned as 'Celebrating Their Freedom' in *The Independent*. What is not clear, as it was glossed over in the coverage of the uprisings, was which part of the population had actually gained their freedom and from whom. Here the young girl can symbolise 'regained innocence' after the war. At the same time this image was taken, Libya was in fact in violent turmoil as different factions struggled for power. But news organisations were not covering this with any emphasis.

We see the same pattern in the photographs of Libya taken by Louis Quail, which appeared in *G2*, the supplement of the British *Guardian* newspaper. Quail is a photographer with many years of experience working for many leading British publications such as *The Sunday Times*, *The Telegraph* and *Marie Claire* but also for international titles, while at the same time doing work for advertising and corporate clients.

Quail pointed out that his photographs reflect the way that picture editors are looking for drama. Out of a choice of images, they will always go for the most dramatic ones. He said that there are many stories that are abstract and complex by nature, and the only way magazines and newspapers can illustrate them is by using portrait shots of the people at the heart of the story.

Figure 1.4 Kids wave the new Libyan flag in Martyr's Square in Tripoli, Libya on the one-year anniversary of the revolution
Source: Michael Graae

The photographs in Figures 1.5 and 1.6 were published in *The Guardian* on Monday, October 29, 2012 titled 'Libya: life after Gaddafi – in pictures' with the strapline 'Photojournalist Louis Quail's reflective and surprisingly affirming images of post-revolution Libya tell the human stories behind the uprisings'.

These very striking, beautiful and moving photographs, we might suggest, are one way by which British readers are taken to the events in Libya. Quail pointed out that national newspapers favour these kinds of personalised images when doing a focus on an event. For papers such as

Figure 1.5   Mother who lost her son in the Libyan conflict
Source: Louis Quail

The Guardian, as opposed to *The Scotsman* above, these striking, yet slightly haunting images are as much part of the newspaper brand as they are merely bearing witness. Such images will be thought through carefully in terms of colour palette, composition and how they sit on the page.

One effect of such images, we could argue, is that they personalise events, often through how they resonate with American–European cultural values. The image of the older woman in the chair in her house with an automatic weapon is jarring for the Western eye. The novel, the quirky, that which places these events into the category of 'difference' is often what attracts a picture editor to particular photographs. The newlywed couple are seen in a post-apocalyptic scene under a broken underpass, in front of a burned-out tank. In both of Quail's images the everyday is placed alongside the unusual and surprising. It is unusual to see children and women depicted with guns. In their study of *National*

Figure 1.6 Married couple, Libya
Source: Louis Quail

Geographic Magazine, Lutz and Collins (1993) pointed to the nature of striking and jarring images that also struck notes with Western values and expectations. Such images would be highly stylised.

As regards Quail's photographs, journalism scholars might argue that they push the reader's understanding of events into the direction of the news frame of 'hope and healing'. Pantti and Wahl-Jorgenson (2007) explain how such dramatic events tend to become ritualised in the news. Disaster coverage typically begins with images fitting the description of 'chaos and destruction', along with personal stories. It then moves on to the 'hope and heroes' news frame, where we hear about survivors and acts of humanity. This is followed by the theme of 'mourning and community', where we are told about moving on and remembering (Turner, 1982). All reporting and images must be located appropriately in this sequence.

The personalisation of stories, as we see above, can also have a role of bearing witness to the destruction and carnage on an everyday level (Pantti and Wahl-Jorgensen, 2007). These are ordinary people living in a real world rather than 'experts'. So they bring a sense of authenticity to the representation of reality. Yet none of these images, we might argue, while carrying these meanings help the reader to understand the complex background and multi-faceted reality of the conflict described.

The local news photojournalist and representing the face of the community

Jonathan Goldberg graduated from Brighton University with a degree in Editorial Photography. When we spoke to him, he was a freelance photographer whose main clients were north London local newspapers such as *Ham&High* and the *Hendon Times*. He has since moved on from local newspaper photography, as people along this career path often do, and his clients now include magazines, agencies and charities. His style of photography has changed accordingly, but we focus here on his early work as a local news photographer and speak to him about the processes involved.

Goldberg explained that freelancing local photographers have very little input on the layout their pictures appear in, the visual style of the publication, the choice of photographs or the type of image they produce. Staff photographers spend more time in the office and develop closer working relationships with the subeditors who are responsible for layout and picture editing. But even then their requests not to crop an image or to choose one image over another aren't always granted. Freelancers, who are rarely in the office and receive their assignments on the phone from picture editors, or from the reporter covering the story, don't know which of their submitted images will be used and how it will be placed or cropped. They merely supply the raw material to be used as is seen fit.

From Goldberg's account, as well as other photojournalists' comments, there appeared to be a general consensus as to what makes a good local news photograph. It wasn't easy for them to put this into words specifically. They rather considered this as something that is simply apparent and commonsense. Goldberg said that local news photographs often show local people involved in local activities. All the pictures are very literal and there's little or no abstraction. If the issue is a burst water main, the image will be of that very water main and a large puddle. There might also be a photo of the very annoyed-looking person whose cellar has been flooded because of the leak. Where there has been vandalism at local shops we will see shopowners looking either shocked or defiant. However, as Goldberg pointed out, it is a challenge to continue to supply the paper with new and interesting takes on stories, which tend to be very routine, cyclical (nativity plays at Christmas, people with ice creams on the first hot day) and repetitive.

He talked about the difference between the nature of the more symbolic photographs required for national newspapers and the authentic images he would be called on to produce for the locals. This can also be seen in the difference between Figures 1.7 and 1.8 taken for an assignment for the closure of a local library. In Figure 1.7 we find young girls

Figure 1.7   A more spontaneous image of a library demonstration
Source: Jonathan Goldberg

Figure 1.8   Suitably posed local-style image of a library demonstration
Source: Jonathan Goldberg

playing around during a demonstration outside the library. Figure 1.8
shows a demonstration on the same issue that took place outside the
High Court in London. The first image appears more symbolic and
suitable for a national newspaper supplement to epitomise life in an
urban neighbourhood. The children are all lost in their own imaginative
worlds. Such almost metaphorical images are typical of magazines such
as *National Geographic* where children are used to represent innocence
and the fundamental shared values of humanity (Lutz and Collins,
1993). Figure 1.8, in contrast, is literal as the participants strike a pose to
show their feelings.

What happens in such images is in fact the reverse of documenting an
authentic moment in time and place. As Goldberg states, these are the
stock images of the visual landscape of the local press. Groups of people
line up showing community responses in clearly marked ways. It is interesting that we have been tutored to see the posed photographs as more
authentic than the more symbolic moment shown in the picture of the
children all lost in their own world, unaware of the gaze of the viewer.

In the local news photograph it is not so much the memorable moment
that replaces the complexity of a situation but typical news frames. Such
moments are in fact the opposite of the memorable. Here the community
makes its views clear on challenges to their quality of life. The newspaper

is able to construe itself as the voice of that community, presenting their concerns with an implied sense of there being a political response. However, news analysts (Bennett, 2005) point out that it will rarely be the case that news coverage will follow up the result of such actions where there is no newsworthy moment to report. In fact the council may not respond and the library remains closed, but this will be unlikely to be found in the press. The same is found at the national level where disaster, famines and conflicts have repeatedly been shown to simply appear in the news without follow up (Cottle, 2009). And likewise closures of libraries will not be analysed in the context of broader political contexts. The local newspaper does not interrogate local society. Rather it attempts to create a representation of this community that can attract sufficient advertising. The photograph, as we have seen in the last two interviews, is one important device through which this is accomplished.

The national newspaper staff photographer: David Levene

David Levene has worked for photography agencies and for major London newspapers such as *The Standard, The Independent* and the *Big Issue*, and now works as a regular contributor to *The Guardian*. He has tended to specialise in portraiture but is also sent on international photoshoots either with a journalist or alone. When *The Guardian* introduced 'Eyewitness' – a double-page spread given over entirely to one or several news photographs – this cemented its visual style and identity, which is built around large-scale, high-quality photography. For the Eyewitness spread national and international photographs are used that document the world on a given day in a unique way. Generally the brief is for the picture to be taken at eye level, to create an all-consuming shot, with everything in focus and wide angle. There must be many details to catch the eye in the foreground, but also points of interest at various distances from the camera. Eyewitness images could reveal a way of life in different parts of the globe or provide insights in relation to a particular issue. Levene has shot many of these. He may be sent abroad for two weeks on another assignment, which may take some time to plan, so he will always be on the look-out for scenes that might work well for the Eyewitness spread to make the most of such trips.

The planning for picture stories would be done with input from people on the picture desk and with the photographer themselves also coming up with ideas. So Levene told us he might work on a theme such as – on one occasion – 'summer in the cities'. For this photographers were sent to every capital city in Europe to produce images that would appear every day all through the month of August. Levene covered a number of cities such as Budapest, Bratislava, Vienna and Ljubljana, with two or three days in each to get the images.

A picture editor might suggest an idea for a photograph. They had heard, for example, that there were hot spas in Budapest where everyone plays chess all day. So Levene spent a few days going to these spas, which he said lent themselves to good images as people were doing something unique and striking for the London news reader in an aesthetically pleasing setting. Levene notes that these images could be seen as cliché travel photography. But there is also an element of documenting every-day life in them as opposed to the purely romantic travel shot. There is also a level of symbolism and abstraction contained in such images that would probably make them unsuitable for a local newspaper.

On other occasions Levene would generate his own images. While in Panama City he had heard talk about the way recession and the drying up of investment had led to the mushrooming of 'ghost towers', unfin-ished high-rise buildings. He had noticed the scene in Figure 1.9 from

Figure 1.9   Eyewitness 'ghost towers' in Panama City
Source: David Levene

the road and saw it as an ideal Eyewitness subject. Here, he said, interest is generated by the activity at the front of the image, the line of the pipe that draws the eye to the background, and the contrast of the boats and mundane everyday life with the failed ambitious developments towering over them.

While such images are clearly stunning, they could be argued to represent, in classic *National Geographic* style, the meeting of different worlds. The past and tradition is juxtaposed with the future and technology. The contrast between the poverty of the slums and the floundering wealth of property speculation is made apparent. But such images do not try to create a depressing view of the world, even when they look on scenes of poverty. They use bright and coordinated colours to provide a lively and adventurous take on humanity. They are designed to invite a response of curiosity rather than shock or outrage in the viewer. But scholars would ask the extent to which such aesthetic scenes, seen with regularity, become part of the background scenery of expected suffering and whether such an 'aestheticisation' of suffering was appropriate. This needs to be seen in the context of photographs, like other visual design resources, being used more systematically and deliberately to communicate specific concepts, ideas, values and attitudes. While this may have been a commonplace strategy in advertising visuals in a former era, editorial visuals have now followed suit. Tom Stoddart mentioned that there was a point when classic black and white photojournalism had started jarring with the advertising contents of the publications it appeared in. Picture editors then actively started looking for imagery that worked better side by side with the glossy and technicolour world of marketing. We examine some of the general changes occurring in news imagery more in later chapters.

Another aspect of Levene's work finds him working alongside journalists. His job in this scenario is to create images to sit alongside a report. An example of this work can be seen in Figure 1.10 from Haiti.

Again we find stylisation in this image, with the saturated and coordinated colours and the beautiful composition. The perspective created by the strong diagonal line of the road and the wooden platform of the cart points the viewer's eye to the mountains in the background. The disaster that is subject of this photo is represented symbolically through unburied corpses, which have clearly been treated unceremoniously. The deformed leg of the old man also points towards poverty and poor health care. He walks on as if dead bodies on a cart were not exceptional. Such images may indeed be stylised. And they have been described as

Figure 1.10   Haiti earthquake, 2010
Source: David Levene

part of the background scenery of routine suffering presented to us by the news media. But presented in context, such images do go beyond the stock patterns generally found in the visual reporting of disasters, further than the token 'bearing witness' where a broken child's toy means disaster. This picture tells a more complex story of a country lacking the resources to simply heal and mend.

Citizen photojournalism

We end this chapter by looking at citizen photojournalism. The picture editors we interviewed had similar views on this kind of photograph, generally relating to the problem of verification. It is assumed that such images can bring new and fresh angles on the world. But at the time of writing it seems that they had already been absorbed by news outlets to fit with the dominant news frames and ritual cycles, as in the case of images produced by the professionals. These photographs too will most likely fall in line with the broader changes occurring in the landscape of journalistic imagery and become part of the more symbolic use of photography.

However, these citizen images can provide visual access to zones where journalists are forbidden or highly restricted. They allow for imagery to come out of Libya, for example, at a point when the photojournalists we considered above were not yet able to gain entry. They also allow for immediacy in coverage of unforeseen attacks or disasters, such as in the case of the photographs taken by the victims of the London bombings as they made their way through the tunnels and smoke. Gillmor (2011) suggests that an optimistic view of these images is that they mean that regimes can no longer assume that they can conceal their brutal acts from the outside world. He notes that the images of Neda Soltani's murder after Iran's rigged 2009 election became a key moment in gaining support for the opposition to the regime.

When Corbis, one of the world's big providers of editorial and creative images, bought Demotix, a syndication organisation for citizen photojournalists, at the end of 2012 it was clear that this form of photograph had become institutionalised as part of the kinds of images that news media carry. Demotix images had appeared on the front pages of *The New York Times*, *The Wall Street Journal* and *The Guardian*, and been used in broadcasts on CNN, NBC and the BBC. Demotix made it possible for anyone to open an account and upload images in a few minutes. Formerly big international image providers like Corbis and Getty required application forms or even lengthy auditioning processes. Demotix at the time had members from around the world, in the Middle East, Asia and across Europe. Corbis was to offer its subscribers a 'curated' selection of Demotix images.

One advantage of organisations like Demotix was that they carried out the work of verification that created the problem for news outlets. But verification can still be problematic (Mortensen, 2011). In the case of the professional photojournalist it is known who they are, that they operate to professional standards and that the origins of the photograph are clear. Both the identity of the photographer and the origins of an image can become problematic if it is sourced through social media. It can be hard to identify who was the original owner of a photograph as it is shared and retweeted. And if the original source cannot be verified, it throws doubt on the value of the photograph itself. An agency must be certain that the content of an image is what it claims to be, and that the person who claims to have taken the image was indeed in a position to do so. There are cases where major news organisations have had to compensate for copyright infringements.

At the time of writing the big agencies such as Associated Press, Reuters and Getty Images, who together provide most of the photographs now used by news organisations, had all developed robust processes for searching social media sites such as Twitter and Facebook when stories were breaking, such as crashes or other events and for dealing with issues such as verification (Keller, 2011). Alan Sparrow, picture editor at the *Metro* newspaper, pointed to the reliance on agencies:

> If the picture is from an unknown source and unlikely to be verified by an agency, it becomes a much bigger issue and the story would have to be quite major to merit the investment in time and effort to stand the story up.

There is also the issue of photographic manipulation. Unlike in newsrooms, citizen photojournalists do not have editors and lawyers examining their work. And this is an era where skilful image manipulation can be done even by children.

Another issue is ethics as it relates to the professional photojournalist's commitment to neutrality and objectivity. First, citizen journalists might not be aware of certain rules that have to be adhered to when taking news pictures. Alan Sparrow told us:

> There are rules that professionals are aware of that amateurs might not be, such as: is there permission to use a picture of someone under 16, has the picture been taken on private property or was there any harassment of the subject?

Secondly, from what we have seen of the work of the professionals in this chapter, while none could be said to manipulate truth, it is clear that all are as interested in capturing moods and ideas and providing images for a market as they are in being objective. But the point here is that the citizen journalist has no such ethics of neutrality. The individual may be thoroughly involved in or motivated by a particular event such as a riot or a conflict. Andén-Papadopoulos and Pantti (2011) argue that such images blur the boundaries between objective observer and the participant with a vested interest. So while the professional may wish to capture the mood or essence of an event, as in Tom Stoddart's photographs of the women surviving in Kosovo, the idea is that they want to show it as it is to the best of their abilities. They don't want to persuade the viewer to take their point of view. The expectation is that the professional journalist will present different sides of an event if they are to be found. A passionate amateur photographer may not. Of course ethics is a complex issue. Both professional and citizen photojournalists will photograph a riot looking to represent those who shout, scuffle or have bloody faces, and not those who look bored or distracted. These are the images that will sell. And one might say that it is the passionate will of photojournalists such as Stoddart coupled with his skill as a photographer that allow him to select moments that give viewers access to the worlds inhabited by others.

Keller (2011) argues that perhaps the biggest problem with images from conflict- or disaster-struck areas is that news organisations may use them as part of signifying on-the-spot news without attempting to provide context. Cushion and Lewis (2010) have made the same criticism of on-the-spot television news footage that adds little to the understanding of events but yet signifies 'liveness', 'immediacy' and being there. We see demonstrators with blood running from their heads, a man and child hiding in rubble from gunfire. Such images are not the same as providing sense and context.

Amateur photojournalism has been thought to give news a new kind of rawness and freshness. It also allows news to have a sense of presenting the perspective of the ordinary person (Andén-Papadopoulos and Pantti, 2011). But Silverstone (2006) argues that visual proximity cannot actually guarantee actual close proximity to events and experiences. This will still depend on the audience's moral engagement with often quite remote others. Allen (2006) suggests there is no guarantee that citizen photojournalism can narrow the gap between news audiences and the lives of strangers around the world. As with the professional images from Libya we looked at earlier in the chapter, such personalised views can easily sit within established news frames.

Cottle (2009) argues that such images will still fall into the context of the established news frames and narratives of major news agencies. Their notions of which events resonate with readers and how they should unfold shape the choice and presentation of images. Citizen photographs in this sense will tend to be used not to create new stories but to provide a greater sense of immediacy for the old formulas of reporting. Researchers have shown that what topics get covered in the first place as regards disasters and conflicts by the global news organisations are those that take place in areas that affect the US and elite countries in terms of investment, tourism or expats. Again, it is likely that citizen-generated images will have to chime with these same news values. Photographs may show close-ups of emotional, shouting people, but they tell us nothing about the nature of the events themselves. Worse, perhaps, their immediacy and rawness suggest that they do.

In this context such images will suffer the same criticisms as the photographs provided by experienced and highly talented professional photographers. They themselves say that images are selected in terms of news frames and the news cycle.

Conclusion

What is clear is that photojournalists don't necessarily work to document reality but rather to sell images. Successful photographers understand the market, as well as having an understanding of what kinds of images are visually appealing and of the rituals and frames of reporting. They also understand the changing nature of how photographs are being used by news outlets and the shift to global syndication. An image that is multi-purpose, that can be used to illustrate a wider range of stories, will simply make more money.

What we would conclude also from this study is that the really important events, that affect us, that drive news events, can't be photographed or at least they are not what news images are about. These things happen in boardrooms such as where NATO politicians agreed to share out Libya's oil. Tanks, smoke, people with guns – unfortunately – make aesthetically interesting photographs, and at the appropriate points in the cycle of reporting. Tenacious young photojournalists like Michael Graae and Louis Quail may well be willing to risk their lives and will return from war zones and refugee camps with more nuanced images, but may simply find them impossible to sell.

And then the question is: should news photos be aesthetically pleasing? Should war look 'beautiful'? All our interviewees felt that this is exactly what photographers are trained to do: look for the stunning shot, the right composition, exciting light and different angles. Were a photograph merely to fulfil its role of bearing witness, things like war may well look boring and certainly not pleasing to the eye. Instead what is more likely to be shown is a woman wailing, standing perfectly framed, with a bit of fire adding drama and the colours just right.

All the photojournalists also agreed that an audience does not linger over badly composed, boring shots. Beauty is what makes us stay around to look at an image. We wouldn't take note of the people in the boardroom. But a child holding a machine gun and a flag in a bleak setting with two exciting colours will have a different effect if we see it at the right time in the news cycle.

Most importantly, we have begun to establish that the photograph is part of the way titles can communicate about their own attitudes to the news. A tabloid can use cut-outs, a quality title can use more ponderous and pleasing, if symbolic images. The image should be thought of in itself as a design resource that can be deployed alongside other elements. While such a claim is nothing new in advertising, it is now increasingly true across different kinds of communicative genres, including news.

2 Magazine Design: Ideas and Attitudes through Visual Elements

In this chapter we begin to look at some of the fundamental features of page design in the form of the use of fonts, colours and photographs. We are specifically interested in how designers work to ensure that magazine content communicates to specific target audiences. Designers make choices concerning visual elements and design features, the way they are positioned and presented, in order to convey specific kinds of ideas and attitudes appropriate to the brand identity of a magazine.

We focus here on print versions of magazines and will discuss online versions in a later chapter. The basic design skills required to put together magazine layouts are still as important today as they were before the advent of online media. On the one hand, the magazine industry has not experienced the decline associated with newspapers and so print-based work is still very much thriving. On the other hand, and perhaps more importantly, such skills carry over in the online and tablet designs we consider in a later chapter.

We begin the chapter with a short introduction on the changing magazine work environment. We then look at the design of the highly successful food magazine *BBC GoodFood*. We use this as an example of how a successful consumer magazine is designed. The task for the designer of this magazine is to locate it precisely in a market that is crammed with competing titles. As we see, this involves signals in terms of photographic elements, font choices and colour as well as kinds of content.

We then move on to look at a very new phenomenon at the time of writing, the availability of ready-made magazine templates that are for sale from online market places where anyone can purchase them. This part of the industry is experiencing massive growth as it allows cost-cutting as publishers can dispense with the need of an in-house designer or the creating of a brief altogether. Here we find designers working creatively to provide ready-made packages into which content can be dropped. While technology may facilitate freedom in one sense, in another it has led to massive templatisation. We use the example of GraphicRiver, a stock library for ready-made print-designs including magazine templates. Templates available on this site, as yet empty of content, are already loaded with design features that carry set ideas and attitudes.

In the following section we look in detail at some of the basic rules for the uses of fonts and colour in magazine design. A detailed analysis of the *GoodFood* design is provided, comparing this with other magazines. In each case we show how multimodal analysis can help us to think more precisely about how detailed design choices communicate to specific markets, looking at some of the general principles of font and colour design.

The chapter ends by bringing together the observations made thus far to see how they apply in the case of the award-winning design for a supplement of the French newspaper *Libération*. We introduce some of the rules for the use of frames and borders, which we develop further in later chapters.

The changing magazine work environment

The introduction of Desktop Publishing (DTP) in the 1980s radically transformed magazine workflow. Prior to that editorial and art departments used to be very separate operations. In many cases the page layouts were done out of house by reprographic companies from words typed up using a word processor, or before that even a typewriter and hard-copy images. The layouts were put onto film – sheets of transparency – and this was used to reproduce the required amount of copies of each page on a printing press. When so-called WYSIWYG (What you see is what you get) page layout software became available, editors and art directors started working together side by side. They produced a digital file of each given layout, which was still initially put onto film. Now the printing process is completely digital and the printing presses produce physical pages straight from a digital file, most commonly a PDF (Portable Document Format) file.

This technology caused massive changes to the production process. Tasks that were previously carried out by highly specialised and skilled people in reprographic companies – preparing pages for the press, assuring colour accuracy, managing typefaces, making sure pages appeared in the right order – are now performed by the editorial staff of magazines. Art directors and production editors now have to manage the workflow of the publication right through to producing a print-ready file, dealing with colour management and quality checks of the files to ensure they won't be rejected by the printers.

Art directors had to learn how to use page layout and image manipulation software, and editors too had to acquire at least a basic understanding of these programs. As control over the visual appearance of magazines has moved in-house and DTP software has become easier to use, the design and look of magazines has grown in importance. More and more research goes into readers' preferences and how the appearance of a magazine is received by its audience. Editors and art directors are now able to shape layouts according to their acquired sense of their readership. Such is the importance of being able to implement an appropriate and successful design that it is not uncommon now for former art directors to be given and take on jobs as editors.

BBC GoodFood magazine

A magazine's front cover is arguably its most important page. A successful cover generates a desire in the reader to pick it up and interact with it. To do this it must communicate the right ideas and attitudes to the intended reader. *BBC GoodFood* magazine uses many specific design details to speak to a specific market group. This case study analyses them and the production processes behind them. We spoke to the art director of the magazine, Andrew Jackson, the brand creative director of *BBC GoodFood*, Elizabeth Galbraith and to Senior Market Insight Executive at BBC Worldwide, Adam Woodgate.

The front cover of *BBC GoodFood* magazine must be able to signal up a particular kind of readership and food experience that distinguishes it from its rivals both at other publishers and as regards the BBC's own other food magazines. *GoodFood* is aimed at a more mature family type of cooking, as opposed to one of BBC's own rival titles, *Olive*, which targets younger professionals.

Work on the cover falls into two distinct categories: work on the image and work on the text elements. The image is the starting point. *BBC GoodFood* magazine has some fundamental rules in place that guide the subject choice for the cover photography. As a food magazine the cover will always show a dish for a recipe in the magazine. The first rule that applies is that savoury dishes will be alternated on the front cover with sweet dishes from one month to the next. Secondly, the type of food shown, as well as the setting in which it is shown, will take into account the time of year and correspond to seasonal events. Another editorial consideration that impacts on the cover image is the theme of the issue. If the issue is about health, there won't be a dessert or cake on the front cover, for example. And in each case the image must communicate a sense of more mature readers who may want to cook for families.

For these rules to be adhered to a twelve-month programme of cover images is roughly mapped out in advance. So rather than picking from any dish imaginable at the beginning of every month there is a suggestion for the dish for every month already in place well ahead of time. Changes and new developments in the course of the year may result in a dish that was planned for the front cover being held over for a month or two or swapped around.

Adam Woodgate told us that a large part of audience research in relation to readers' reactions to visuals is focused on the front cover. Sales revenue trends suggest that *BBC GoodFood* magazine sells particularly well with either roast chicken or chocolate on the front cover. The readership awareness department at Immediate Media (formerly BBC Magazines) puts the latest issues of the magazine in front of a reader panel about four times a year. So-called 'heat maps' are used to determine which part of the cover is particularly attractive to readers. These are generated by bringing up a cover on a screen and instructing members of the reader panel to click on the area of the cover that first attracted their eye. The clicks are then used to colour the cover in shades of yellow to red, getting darker with a higher number of clicks. Feedback from the readership department also includes readers' likes or dislikes towards certain colours and fonts.

The process of producing the front cover of *BBC GoodFood* magazine will usually start with a meeting between the food editor, the editor and the art director. Andrew Jackson, the art director, said: 'You sit down and discuss what's looking good from the issue, what recipes we'd like to see, what the theme of the issue is, what would be strong, what colours we would like to see on it.' The editor might use a descriptive phrase to give the designer an idea of the overall feel they would like to aim for with the cover layout. For the February 2012 cover, the catch-phrase the editor used was: 'A splash of sunlight on a dull day.' He said that this immediately conjures up a fairly clear idea of what the desired visual experience is going to be: it suggests a washed-out background with very light and cool colours, and in contrast to that a dish that is bright and vibrant, with very warm inviting colours.

For a chosen dish several different versions will be made after some discussion as to what it might look like. So, for example, if the chosen cover dish of the month is a cheesecake, the test kitchen adjacent to the editorial office might prepare three different kinds of cheesecake for the art director to see. These can then all be photographed, and Jackson will choose the one that lends itself best to be shown on a cover, because of its texture or colour. Upon viewing the finished dish in the test kitchen the art director might also ask for amendments to be made to the dish. For the rice dish on the February 2012 cover, for example, it was felt that it would look more colourful and vibrant if it had more turmeric and more red peppers in it. The original recipe contained chicken, which was replaced by prawns, Jackson said, 'because prawns are more graphic, they stand out more'.

With a clear picture in his mind about what the dish will look like, Jackson prepares several sketches of how this dish may sit within the composition of the cover and what other elements may appear in the photograph. These sketches are used both in further discussion with the editor about the cover and to brief the prop stylist and the photographer.

The sketches (Figure 2.1) are useful in giving a tangible idea about how a given dish will work in the context of a front cover. Several compositions for the photograph can here be explored before the actual shoot takes place. The masthead, words and secondary images can be added in to see how they might fit in with the image. Notes alongside the sketches record thoughts and options the designer has in mind, such as the feel and colouring of the surface the dish will be presented on, potential props and the proportional size of the food shown in the picture.

The team then need to tell the prop stylist what other elements are needed for the image, such as table, plates, etc. Jackson said they take pictures of the food from the test-kitchen and then send these along with the cover sketches via email. They will also get the recipe title, description and the sizes, dimensions and kind of feel he is looking for. They will then look around for a number of possibilities and will know the kinds of shops that would provide the right kinds of props.

The January 2012 front cover contained certain kinds of plates that were felt to be perfect for the specific market. Jackson said: 'The stylist got these round tiles [porcelain serving tiles]. The detail on them is very

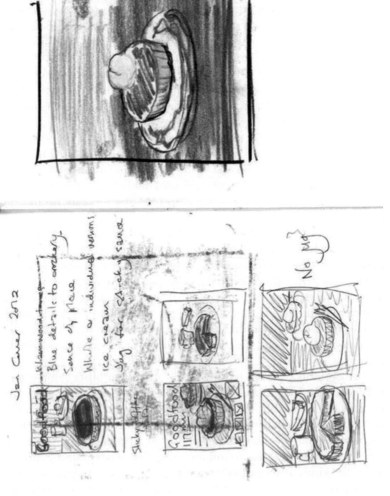

Figure 2.1   GoodFood sketches

subtle, but it's there, it's not as strong as it is on this [sketch], but it's there. You can see it.' Elizabeth Galbraith added:

> What's happening here is that you are creating an atmosphere in the image. So this blue detail says, it's a little bit special. It also brings a bit of colour into the image. Otherwise this would all be shades of brown. It's slightly decorative, too. There are other ways you could [tell the same story], but the first way is to think what is the tart served on. If you wanted it to look like a party, you would have it on something silver – quite bright and shiny, because that says 'party'.

The art directors get a good idea of whether the photo-shoot has the desired results at the time. But they only really know how successful an image is once they've taken all the shots back to the office and incorporated them into the cover layout. Sometimes it is at this stage that the decision is made to reshoot the image and the team will have to go back into the photo studio to start again. The January 2012 *BBC GoodFood* cover is one case that had to be shot again (Figure 2.3). Galbraith said that on average maybe two *Olive* covers a year have to be reshot. Often this is because the composition just doesn't look strong enough once text and other features are added.

Figure 2.2 Two versions of the same *GoodFood* cover with different images and insert shapes

Figure 2.3   Actual *GoodFood* cover that was used

Semiotics of magazine design

We can think a little more systematically about the *GoodFood* composition by drawing on Barthes' two-step analysis. This is a form of semiotic analysis that is useful for identifying all elements and features in an image and for specifying the exact role they play in communication. Barthes was interested in two levels of meaning in images. On one level images can be said to document. In the case of a magazine cover we can simply ask what is *depicted* or *denoted*, such as a car, an antique plate, a milk jug.

At the second level elements and objects will be used to get general or abstract ideas across or to *connote* ideas and concepts. So we can ask what kinds of identities, actions and values are associated with a particular kind of car, antique plate or milk jug.

The iconography of the January edition of *GoodFood* magazine shows two small cupcakes arranged with one in the foreground and the other further away in the background, to the right. This creates a sense of cooking not so much for many people but rather for two people. In Figure 2.2 above we can see that one of the designs that was rejected carries the larger cake with a slice taken out of it. It suggests a larger family event. The designer told us that in this case the aim was more towards a smaller, intimate kind of dish. Galbraith said that this would be in contrast to *Olive*, which was for the younger reader interested in cooking for groups of friends. Within *Olive* magazine it is common to see younger people sitting in designer apartments and to find wine and travel features. *Olive*, she said, was more about cooking as a lifestyle, so as part of an appreciation of restaurants, travel and food and designed dishes. *Olive* magazine, she said, was for a generation that have learned about food not from their mother but from eating out in cities. This can be seen on the cover in Figure 2.4.

Importantly, on the *GoodFood* cover the plate and the fork are not new or modern, as we might find in *Olive*, but are the sort of thing obtained from a grandmother or found in a second-hand shop, although these are

Figure 2.4   Olive magazine cover, with its cooking and lifestyle look

tasteful, as opposed to simply old. Along with the table there is a sense of something rustic and the cosy of the traditional. The cake is beautifully made, and there is a sense of lavishness and luxury in the way the icing sugar is scattered around the plate onto the brown tablecloth and the caramel dribbles down onto the plate. The cloth itself appears to be soft and velvety. There is a sense of warmth and luxury here. In *Olive* we find pictures of upmarket celebrity chefs, exteriors and interiors of top restaurants and wine shops. There is also a greater number of images of food shown in airy kitchens or dining interiors as opposed to close-ups of plated food on tables. The cover of *Olive* in Figure 2.4 uses a more modern fine-dining-shaped transparent serving dish. In its sleekness this almost evokes a sense of the futuristic. Settings can comprise highly modernist polished surfaces, bright white loft spaces for breakfast ideas, and even budget kitchen settings – although with more tasteful and classic selected 'cheap' furniture. There are images of groups of young people or young families eating out in restaurants.

In fact across these two magazines there is some crossover of looks and certainly of recipes. But what is important is the way that cooking and recipes are presented in the context of particular connotations about lifestyle and brand. They reflect certain identities, of family or young and fashionable friends, of cooking skills and appreciation of good cooking or more contemporary, sleeker restaurant-type looks with minimalist plates and settings.

Ready-made magazine templates

In the previous chapter we spoke a little about stock libraries for photographs. We mentioned how photojournalists will tend to submit to these libraries images that are multi-purpose, that can be used creatively by magazine and newspaper editors around the world cheaply and conveniently. One criticism of these was that such generic images tend to be more symbolic than documentary. It makes photographs become more aligned with design and style rather than being authentic documents that bear witness to an immediate and specific situation. Images become typical and multi-purpose rather than original. More recently similar online market places for other graphic design elements have begun to emerge. It is now possible to buy all kinds of page design elements, from illustrations, charts, logos and icons, to entire magazine templates complete with fonts, colour scheme and layout, for an editor to simply fill in text and pictures. Prices for the templates start from as little as $3 if the buyer intends to use it to create a product for free distribution. If the buyer is planning on using the template to put together a magazine to be sold to readers, a different kind of licence is required and the cost is considerably higher. A growing number of online sites offer this kind of magazine template. We looked more closely at a site called graphic-river.net.

GraphicRiver is part of a wider network of related sites for creative output called Envato, which, at the time of writing, has around 3 million registered users. Buyers aren't obliged to register, so the actual number of users may be higher still. Designers supply GraphicRiver with material, and it is interesting to note, scrolling through the list of their profiles, that by and large they are based in the Balkans and the Far East.

We interviewed several of the designers to better understand the process of designing generic magazines. In this case they do not follow a particular magazine brand's brief, as would be the case in the previous examples. Rather, the process involves creating a design that would potentially be used by different clients, for different audiences and contexts and in different environments.

The designers pointed out that it was very liberating to be free to create a look they liked without the interference of a client who may have a poor understanding of design yet want to have their ideas incorporated. Some felt that on the whole the templates on GraphicRiver are of a much higher quality than actual magazine designs available on the news stand simply because they are not the result of compromises between designers and clients with an editorial agenda. One designer poignantly stated that producing templates for GraphicRiver represents a role-reversal. Instead of the designer being hemmed in by a client's brief, the designer gives clients the basis to be creative themselves, but the client in turn was limited by the parameters that the designer sets within the template.

Others pointed out that this perceived freedom came at a price. Designs have to be easy to use, even for someone with very little experience of the InDesign software. All the required stylesheets, which pre-set the different kinds of font and paragraph characteristics found on any given page, have to be in place. All design elements have to be executed in very simple ways. If files do not fulfil those requirements, they don't pass the GraphicRiver quality control. Even if they do pass the quality control, they might result in bad reviews from users, thereby curtailing their resale value. Factors such as usability and good reviews are of major importance when any given design can sell for as little as $3. It will only be worth a designer's while if it sells several times, and sometimes a good design sells a thousand times over.

The designers develop various strategies to help them generate higher repeat sales for a given design. While each template is very much fixed, the designs can contain flexibility. A template may, for example, include several different colour palettes from which different clients can choose to create considerably different products. But template designers also think about wider values and ideas being communicated by specific design features that are suitable for different market groups. In practice this leads to fairly high levels of predictability in the use of these design features. A search in the database for a term like 'extreme' will throw up designs with angular, heavy fonts, saturated colours and overlapping images, texts and graphics. Searches under 'technology' or 'innovation' will also throw up designs containing standard characteristics and patterns that readers recognise to fit into those categories. These will then find their way into publications around the planet. Magazine templates lead to greater standardisation of design patterns around the world.

What is clear from these templates, as newspaper designer Michael Crozier suggests, is that they are part of a major transformation in print design. It has becomes more sophisticated and deliberate. Close attention is paid to how image type, content and placement can be used alongside and integrated into text to point to the identity and meaning of the product. The business magazine template in Figure 2.5 is a good example of this. Topics are typical of contemporary business philosophy, with notions of 'inspiration' and 'dreams' being foregrounded, already inviting particular kinds of content. Visual features too point to mobility and lightness. Fonts are modern, light and well spaced, to suggest room to think and breathe. Attention has been given to creating white space. Colour has been used to create rhyme on each page and also across pages as colour boxes are themselves added to give mood but also link to images across the page. The teardrop shape of the box recurs throughout this magazine template and is a good example of how the playfulness of online design has now filtered into the work of print designers too (Cousins, 2012a). This is not a business magazine that communicates ruthlessness, aggression or stress, but 'forward thinking', 'open minded' and 'innovation' where business can be easily aligned with style and culture. Such a design will be used to communicate these ideas and values around the world.

Figure 2.5 Business magazine template 'Inspiration' page

As with stock libraries for photographs, these template libraries represent the possibility for visual design to become increasingly generic. All design relies on clichés to some extent, but this invites massive repetition of generic renderings of sets of ideas and values around particular subjects such as business, interior design and extreme sports. While larger organisations will still create their own unique designs, template designers will copy their most attractive elements and amalgamate them into designs that have high aesthetic appeal, but due to their versatility will have a somewhat flat meaning potential. They become increasingly interchangeable. In themselves many will probably be used for free in-house circulation within companies and organisations such as universities and hospitals, where staff news will be delivered wanting to communicate ideas of 'inspiration' and 'dreams'. But as media organisations suffer from commercial pressures they, too, may start to turn to cheaper design solutions. In Chapter 4 we turn our attention to where there is evidence that this has begun to take place, particularly in the online environment.

The rules for font and colour in visual design

In the Introduction we mentioned scholars around the turn of the 21st century observing a change in communicative modes and how they were used to systematically convey ideas and attitudes. Our analysis of the choice of props on magazine covers has corroborated this. Now we turn our attention to fonts and colour. Designers themselves explain their decisions in terms of aesthetics and through less specific adjectives. A designer may intuitively say that a design is 'fun' or 'warm', without knowing exactly what features and elements create this feel. We suggest theoretical models that can be used to better understand and analyse design decisions. We draw in particular on the work of Van Leeuwen (2005) and Machin (2007).

Multimodal analysis of fonts

First we systematically examine the use of fonts in *BBC GoodFood*, comparing them with those used in other magazines.

Fonts can fulfil the three meta-functions that we explained in the Introduction. First, they communicate ideas. So a thicker-looking typeface can suggest the idea of something stronger or more robust as opposed to a very thin one, which can suggest something weaker or slight. Second, fonts can communicate attitudes. So typefaces can be bold and assertive, or small, dainty and thoughtful. Third, fonts can be used to create hierarchies and links on a page. All of these three are used more systematically in contemporary design.

There are eight basic font qualities that combine within one typeface to fulfil these three functions and contribute to the font's overall meaning.

1. Weight

This is about how bold or heavy a font appears. Bold can mean daring, assertive, solid and substantial and its opposite, timid or insubstantial. But boldness can have negative meanings and suggest something overbearing or domineering. Lack of weight can suggest subtleness or lightness. We can see these differences if we compare the typeface for the magazine names on *GoodFood* and *delicious* (Figure 2.6). *GoodFood* is heavier and suggests something substantial, while *delicious* looks lighter and more delicate. It conveys elegance and possibly a hint of luxury and exquisiteness. A different kind of magazine, such as for cars, may use an even heavier font, which can be indicative of boldness of attitude.

New look!

delicious.

ON SALE 1-28 FEBRUARY 2014 £3.90   deliciousmagazine.co.uk

**85 reasons
to love ♡
February**
● Cosy recipes from
the Bake Off kitchens
● Comfort food
for Duvet Day

let's eat!
Wise ways to
make midweek
meals stress-free

Plus...
● Vegetarian tagines
...and more
● Energy-boost smoothies
● Lorraine Pascale's
better-for-you bakes
● Slow-roast pork

Secret
ingredient:
Rolos

Seduction
on a plate
Easy menu
for two

better
cook
12 pages of expert advice
● Step by step: croissants
● Expert guide: seville
orange marmalade
● How to make a
sourdough starter

*Mmmmm...
brownies*

Figure 2.6 *delicious* magazine cover

2. Expansion

Typefaces may be condensed and narrow, or they may be expanded. Maximally condensed typefaces make maximal use of limited space. This can mean that they are precise and economical or even discreet. Wide typefaces, in contrast, spread themselves around, using space as they wish, making their presence felt. The values of this may be reversed. Widely spread typefaces may be seen in a positive light as providing room to breathe, while condensed typefaces might be seen as cramped, overcrowded or restrictive of movement. Letter expansion can also be used to affect the pacing of a magazine. Using condensed lettering can also give the impression of greater haste – of fitting more information into a smaller space – which creates a similar effect to speaking fast and saying more in a shorter period of time. Using extended fonts slows things down and gives the reader time and space to think.

The *GoodFood* masthead uses a slightly condensed font. This may be appropriate for suggesting a degree of economy. Were the font to be expanded it may also give a sense of the food being too heavy. In contrast, we can see that *Olive* uses slightly more spacing, perhaps suggesting greater room for ideas and creativity.

3. Slope

This refers to the difference between cursive, sloping, script-like typefaces and upright typefaces as characterised by print, but also to the difference between italicised and regular fonts. Slope can be right or left leaning. The meaning potential here is based on the association of handwriting and printing – between something straight and regular and something more informal and slanted. Script fonts are more personal, informal, handcrafted and can suggest oldness. They can suggest an individual writer addressing the reader personally as opposed to an institution addressing the public at large. Their curliness can also come across as very feminine, and they are more likely to appear in magazines with a predominantly female readership. Regular serif or sans serif fonts are more mechanical, impersonal, formal and new. They convey greater authority and factualness while script fonts are more poetic.

The difference between regular and script fonts can also mean the difference between something solid and lasting as opposed to something more impermanent. A handmade product may use a written typeface to suggest something personal and potentially short-lived.

Slope can also be used to suggest something dynamic and energetic. This is particularly true when the italicised version of a regular font is used. This creates the impression of something accelerating, with the top part of the letters moving off at speed ready to pull their bottom parts along, which for the moment remain inert. Italicisation is otherwise used to make the names of artworks, books, films and plays stand out in running copy while avoiding the use of intrusive inverted commas. When whole paragraphs are set in italics, however, it can create a similarly informal, lighter, less serious effect. Comments added by the editor at the end of articles are often set in italics.

4. Curvature

Letterforms can stress angularity or they can stress curvature. They can, of course, mix the two. The significance of these may be based on experiential and cultural associations with round and angular objects. Roundness can suggest soft, smooth, natural and organic, whereas angularity can suggest harshness, be aggressive, technical or masculine (Garfield, 2011). Both may be positively or negatively valued. Angularity and straight lines are also associated with rationality and modernity, whereas postmodernism has brought curvature back into design.

We can see that the *delicious* name uses a highly rounded typeface, suggesting something softer and more natural perhaps. Even the serifs, as seen at the top of the 'd' are slightly rounded-off as opposed to the sharper ones on the *Gardens Illustrated* font as seen in Figure 2.7. This sits alongside its subtlety and space to breathe. We could imagine that this font could be used for an organic product pointing to a rounded, well-balanced diet. In contrast, the *GoodFood* title font is for the most part rounded if we compare it to *Gardens Illustrated*. While it is not as rounded as *delicious*, it is certainly not angular, harsh or technical.

5. Connectivity

Letter forms can be connected to each other, as in running handwritten script, almost touch each other, or even be pressed together. Or they can appear separate and self-contained. Where letters are further apart this might suggest isolation, disconnection or even fragmentation. It evokes a sense of individuality, space to think and room to move. Where letters are closer together it can connote integration, wholeness and unity. There has been a trend in newspapers to use slightly greater spacing between letters to create a sense of room to think, giving space for opinions. The formerly used compact typefaces signalled up the newspaper as a more dogmatic traditional informer of the public.

The *delicious* title uses letters that are slightly further apart. Along with curvature, softness and the lower case suggesting subtlety and moderation, spacing also suggests room to think and opinions. This points to meanings associated with the magazine's particular target reader, who may be more inclined towards dining out, regarding cooking as lifestyle rather than part of a daily routine. The letters of *GoodFood* are much more closely placed and suggest wholeness and a unity of purpose. It creates the impression that the publication places value on and foregrounds tight-knit relationships, belonging and warmth.

6. Direction

Typefaces can be oriented towards the horizontal dimension by being comparatively flattened, with equal or even greater width than height.

Or they can be stretched in the vertical direction where height is greater than width. Flatter fonts can appear more stable but also seem heavy and inert. Tall, slim fonts can suggest aspiration and loftiness, but also pompousness and self-satisfaction. *GoodFood* has a slight sense of tallness, rather than flatness, which helps to give a sense of aspiration.

7. Regularity

Some typefaces have irregularities or features that appear random. So letters may be different sizes, widths, shapes. Or they may be simply positioned at slightly different heights from the line. Regularity and irregularity too have their meaning potential. We often find irregularity in advertisements for products for younger children. This can suggest fun or playfulness as opposed to the formal regularity of letters. It might also point to a lack of conformity or even wackiness or craziness. On food magazines we tend not to find wackiness or non-conformity.

8. Flourishes

Letters can have a range of flourishes and additions that can also carry meaning potential. These might comprise loops and swirls to communicate energy, flamboyance or lightness, or may include iconographic imagery. One important flourish is the 'foot' of the serif. These are originally related to alignment of letters but now tend to connote tradition. Where they are not present there is more of a sense of modernity. A plaque for a government official's office will tend to use serifs.

The *GoodFood* cover does not use flourishes. In this sense it is more modern than what we find, for example, for the *Gardens Illustrated* magazine.

Multimodality and colour design

It is possible to analyse colour choices on the two covers similarly systematically. Again the first step is to point out that colour can fulfil three meta-functions.

First, colour can communicate ideas. A colour can connote a nation, the idea of science (usually blue), or summer (usually yellow). Second, colours communicate attitudes. Bright or saturated colours can be used to draw our attention to them. More muted colours communicate more subtle moods. Pure colours communicate greater levels of certainty than impure colours. Third, colours can be used to create hierarchies and links on a page, to create links between objects, logos and texts. This may be done not only by hue but also by other colour qualities such as degrees of saturation or dilution. Different elements on the page can be linked as they share the same degree of colour saturation. As with fonts we can list a number of colour qualities that can be harnessed to fulfil these meta-functions. Six of these follow.

1. Brightness

The meaning potential of brightness relates to our experience of light and dark. Darkness is associated with secrecy, ignorance, concealment, lies, depression and even the irrational and primitive. Light is associated with openness, truth, reason and optimism. Intense brightness can go further to mean purity, spiritual vision, even other-worldliness, whereas dark and shadow can mean evil. Often advertisements use high-key lighting to give the places and persons they represent a soft brightness, which brings almost a sense of spirituality.

The *GoodFood* cover combines darker, although mainly warmer, colours with the use of bright highlights for the food itself, which is both front- and back-lit, making it vibrant. The white powder on the tablecloth also helps to increase brightness. The brightness on the food links with the whiteness of the drop box at the bottom right and the white text across the top of the cover and to the bottom left. The plate also contains a bright light-blue, and there are bright turquoise fonts. So while there is the darkness of the winter we also find cosiness, optimism and energy. Even on their seasonal cover rival title *Olive* uses the brightness of a luminous turquoise background. This chimes more with the younger lifestyle market than the cosy fireside feel. The *delicious* cover contrasts the brightness of white fonts with a darker background and picture subject, giving it a strident, modern feel.

2. Saturation

There is a scale from intensely saturated colours to very dilute versions of these colours where they become paler and pastel, or even dull. The associations of the saturation level relate to emotional temperature. Richly saturated colours suggest intensity of feeling, exuberance, adventure and vibrancy. Dilute colours can mean subtle, tender or even moody. There can be negative meanings. Saturated can mean showy, vulgar and garish, whereas dilute can mean dull, lacking in energy, moody.

The flowers on many *Gardens Illustrated* covers typically make use of a high level of saturation, making them very exuberant and sensory. The green of the surrounding foliage is often highly saturated, emphasising the idea of vivacity, the beauty of nature, the environment and the sort of well-tended garden a *Garden Illustrated* reader might appreciate used on this cover. The saturated greens and deep purples form a beautiful contrast.

The *GoodFood* cover uses a highly saturated colour for the main title font and the colours on the cake – the caramel and the cream are saturated, enhanced digitally in the retouching process that is applied to the photograph. It brings a sense of richness and exuberance to the food presented here.

The *Olive* cover uses the most obviously saturated colours of the cover samples shown. A bright blue background offsets a glowing orange masthead. It is fun and adventurous for gatherings of friends. Its measure of reserve comes from the very simple pared-down cover photograph rather than from using dilute colours.

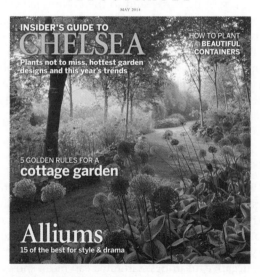

Figure 2.7   Gardens Illustrated magazine cover

3. Purity

Colours can be maximally pure or highly hybrid. The terms 'pure' and 'hybrid' themselves suggest the meaning of this quality. Purity means certainty, simplicity, clean, whereas hybridity can mean complex, uncertain, ambiguity.

The *GoodFood* cover uses the brown of the table surface, the blue and white of the plates, all of which are pure. The main title is set in a pure pink and the same goes for the turquoise subtitles. While we find similar colours for the *Olive* cover, the turquoise of the background appears to become darker in places and in others suffused with white. This is of interest given the magazine's target readers who are younger and may relate more to postmodern sentiments. The *delicious* title appears in the same colour every month, with a particular method using silver foil. The foil can bring connotations of modern spaces with reference to the use of polished steel in contemporary designs. It also generates a sense of elegance and possibly even of something a little bit precious.

4. Modulation

Colours can be fully modulated, where we can see rich textures with different tints and shades as light falls and creates different shades of that particular hue. But they can also be unmodulated and flat, as we might find in a cartoon. Flat unmodulated colours are seen as simple and bold, or as overly basic. Highly modulated colours can appear as more naturalistic and documentary as they point to complexity. Heightened modulation is often used in photography to connote gritty realness and revealing of truth.

On the *GoodFood* cover we find extremely high modulation for the food. While these are highly staged and designed images, this high modulation helps to communicate realism. On other magazine covers such as *Cosmopolitan* we might find a woman represented where colours of her clothing, hair and skin have reduced modulation. In this case it is clear that she has been somehow simplified and idealised. This is important on such lifestyle titles where the women in the pages represent not real persons but generic types of seductive, assertive women. On food magazines the settings often have reduced modulation and flatter colours. They are simplified in order to symbolise particular lifestyles whereas the food has increased modulation and connotes the heightened realness and sensory nature of the food's textures and flavours.

5. Differentiation

This is the scale that runs from monochrome, where there are only different tones of one single colour, to a highly varied colour palette. The use of a large range of colours can mean fun, adventure, liveliness, energy, diversity. The use of lower levels of differentiation can mean moderation, restraint, timelessness or old-fashionedness. There can also be negative connotations, in which a large palette means garish and unrestrained whereas a restricted palette means dull and suppressed, lacking energy and fun.

GoodFood magazine will use a greater palette to help to bring life to the cover. Fonts are usually set in only two or three different colours to avoid unnecessary confusion and so one of the colours can serve a highlighting function. These will be experimented with until there is a sense of balance, as shown by the differentiation in the cover lines and masthead in Figure 2.3. The *delicious* cover is restrained in colour palette, pointing to a sense of measure and sophistication.

6. Hue

This is about the meanings of the colours themselves. Here is the scale that runs from the warmth of reds used for energy, salience and fore-grounding to the coolness of blues used for science and truth, calmness or distance. Blue hues are often used in corporate branding. Other colours, by association, are better for communicating natural things such as greens and browns. These colours can also be used to represent tradition and history due to associations with the land. Yellow is used for brightness and optimism. White and blues can mean purity and white can mean clean and ordered. Lilacs are feminine. Of course the meaning of a hue will always be construed from its combination with the other colour characteristics described above. A red may be warm and saturated or dilute and impure.

On the *GoodFood* cover we have feminine colours such as pink and turquoise along with browns for tradition and history and whites for cleanliness. The bright and energetic yellow of the trial cover has been removed in the final version. The range of hues on the *Olive* cover is similar but without the browns connoting tradition. The hybrid turquoise it uses points to femininity but also to something highly contemporary.

Framing and page rhythm

We end this chapter with an exploration of page composition. One important aspect of design is the way elements are allowed to relate to each other, whether they are grouped together within frames or segregated by borders. We spoke to Javier Errea about his design practice. He told us about his work for the French newspaper *Libération*. Errea said that creating two kinds of reading rhythm was important with this title. These were *paused* reading and *condensed* reading. The difference can be seen between the layouts in Figures 2.9 and 2.10. One clearly has a section of text to be read and the other elements dispersed across the page. This strategy shapes the reading experience for the audience of the magazine. But it is also an important part of communicating the ideas and attitudes of the title. *Libération* has a fascinating history from its origins in the late 1960s, being launched as a radical left-wing title by Jean-Paul Sartre. Until the 1990s it maintained a strong position for its left-wing views, although commentators say that it ceased to be really radical from the 1970s. Later the title experienced financial difficulties and has gradually shifted to centre left. Visually the title still communicates a sense of taking an intellectual, critical view of the world, even if this has long ceased to be the radical stance of the 1970s. Part of how the title now communicates its identity is through the two reading rhythms. And this is partly accomplished by framing.

Framing is to do with elements being represented as separate or related units. The degree of flow around a page, and certainly of connection between elements, can be indicated by framing. One way of thinking about how frames work is through the association with thickness and strength of boundaries such as walls. Thicker walls suggest more of a barrier than a thin one. Elements can also be separated by space, which, designers say, gives them room to breathe. Elements might overlap, which allows them to share meaning. In recent newspaper designs cut-out images often overlap slightly into the masthead. In traditional tabloid designs such as magazines like *Closer*, feature and news elements can all overlap. In these cases meanings are shared and blended to different degrees.

Here are the ways that elements can be positioned as regards framing:

- Segregation: Elements are separated by a frame, occupy different domains and are therefore of a different order. There will be frames of varying thickness. The thickness of the frame can indicate the strength of the segregation between elements. These frames contain elements that are to be kept apart, indicating

(continued)

that they are of a different order. A magazine cover like *Gardens Illustrated* uses a border to segregate its title from its contents. We can also see this in the case of *Libération*, which uses a very fine delicate line. Designer Errea told us that some more masculine traditional titles were heavy on borders, which brought a sense of order and regulation.

- Separation: Elements can also be separated by empty space. There is no physical border. In this case the elements on either side have some similarity but some differences since they are kept apart. There are no boundaries to cross, only space. We can think of the way that a news headline is separate, but connected to, the text that follows.
- Integration: In this case elements occupy the same space. Images can be placed in the space occupied by the text, or text can be placed over an image. Here these elements can share meaning, or operate as one element.
- Overlap: This is where elements cross boundaries or seep into other spaces. Here rather than in integration we have 'bleeding' of meaning. The element that has the ability to leave its frame is shown as being unrestricted by the conventions of the composition. In Figure 2.10 we see that there are frames on the *Libération* page, but that these are freely overlapped. This is important for indicating freedom of thought.
- Rhyme: Elements within frames, or across different frames, can be linked through some common quality. This might be through shape or colour, for example. We see in the page of *Business* magazine that the depicted people are given frames of the same size, which are separated but not segregated. Different-sized frames and actual borders would create a hierarchy or a sense of difference.
- Contrast: Elements may be differentiated through colour or size. Frame size and shape itself can be used to create contrast or rhyme. In Figure 2.9 the image of Berlusconi is used to create contrast. In fact across the design of *Libération* Errea said that great value is placed on contrast. This too signals a kind of attitude.
- Iconography: Of course frame shape and style can carry meaning. Frames may have straight, jagged or rounded, soft edges, for example. They may also have iconographical qualities such as animal tracks or film reel.

In the case of *Libération* we find two kinds of patterns of framing for the two reading rhythms the designer is seeking. In Figure 2.9 there is no overlap. Segregation is used to create large areas of luxurious space around quite a condensed section of text. Contrast between frame sizes is nevertheless brought in to create interest. There is little segregation from one image to another, creating a sense of intimacy between them. This is a different kind of intimacy from that of the tabloid composition where images may be cropped and overlapped to impose a more literal kind of narrative.

In Figure 2.10, in contrast, we find integration and overlap. We can see that the letter 'a' overlaps the fine borders and the photograph to the bottom left. The headline text overlaps everything. But to some extent this overlap is measured and obeys the lines of other elements. The text, for example, follows the line of the letter 'a'.

Overall design in Libération

Framing, of course, sits alongside the other kinds of design elements that we have considered so far in this chapter.

In terms of imagery *Libération* makes frequent use of cut-outs, extreme close-ups or pictures that suggest movement. Errea said that he had pushed editors to cease to think of the photograph as simply accompanying the text or as a literal illustration of an aspect of the story the article tells, but to think more about the photograph's own narrative power, its ability to communicate emotion and energy. In Errea's words this means practically that images of persons are chosen in order to highlight actions and reactions rather than being a pure indicator of who they are. It also means that the point of view offered to the viewer will be less flat. Layouts can create interest through employing more creative points of view, or where photographs involve the viewer in the scene depicted. In the Introduction we saw an example of how the viewer becomes a witness to a scene from the point of view of one of the participants.

As regards choices in typography Errea said that in the last redesign they had reduced the use of modern fonts to go back to more classic typefaces. He described them as 'quiet' fonts, such as Glosa. This is a delicate font with elegant serifs. He said that there was some surprise when he had wanted to introduce this particular font, as it was part of the magazine's design of the 1990s and had gone out of use generally. But here its gentle emotional curves operate differently when placed in the more modernist space of contemporary designs. The font will also be used at different sizes, often placed together, communicating creativity and non-conformity.

Glosa is combined with Neutraface, designed by the modernist architect Richard Neutra, giving an Art Deco look, seen in the word 'weekend' on the cover and also in the contents above (Figure 2.8). This font is known for its quirky low centre of gravity where the horizontals sit low down on the 'E' and 'F'. In use it also brings possibilities for sharp angles combined with larger curves on the upper case 'P'. It is common to see this used in the magazine where lower case letters appear at the low centre of gravity next to upper case letters. Set alongside Glosa and placed in contemporary design, this is also useful for pointing to style awareness, thoughtfulness and creativity. The Neutra font sits over and combines well with the tall and aspirational font used for the 'Libération' title.

Finally, for the body text a typically modern font by Christian Schwartz is used. So while the other two fonts are highly unusual in their combination, this is more commonplace in modern publishing. Clean and uncluttered fonts that combine both angularity and curvature are very much in vogue. Errea said that the fonts are slightly condensed. This is also of note. In the next chapter we find many newspaper designers talking about the shift to creating more space between letters. Here, however, we find the contrasts between space, paused reading, contrasted with more dense sections. These more condensed fonts, as seen in the title for the 'Miyazaki' item, create a sense of economy of space rather than spreading out and taking up of space.

One of the authors was recently working on corporate brochures, which tended to use more spread-out fonts. While the brochures spoke of having vision, commitment, being competitive and ambitious in a demanding market, visually there was, in contrast, a sense of ease, the luxury and power of space and soothing colours. Sections of text and photographs of employees were given huge amounts of space to spread out.

Colour is also important in the *Libération* design. The different types of contents are given a theme colour, such as aubergine for books, green for cinema.

The photographs used on the pages themselves will carefully avoid wide colour palettes, although it is common to find several bright, exciting colours. The titles will add one highly saturated splash at the top of the page, pointing to the values of entertainment. The cover in Figure 2.8 uses an electric, highly saturated red, the brand colour for

Figure 2.8 Illustrated cover of a 2014 edition of *Libération* magazine

Libération, an emotionally intense, pure, certain colour. Of note in this design is that the saturated colours in the cartoon have been taken for the fonts in the contents that lie at the top of the composition, resulting in a certain degree of rhyming but also creating a sense of a wider colour palette and therefore of fun and playfulness.

74

Figure 2.9   *Libération*: condensed reading page

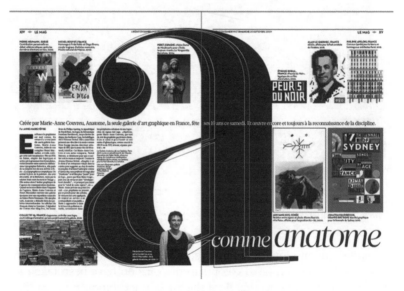

Figure 2.10   *Libération*: paused reading page

Conclusion

There have been huge changes in production processes in the magazine industry as new technology has become established. What we have seen in this chapter is the attention to detail that is used to indicate specific niche market positions. Even though content may be very similar to other titles, they are framed differently to communicate ideas and attitudes about the given subject and the specific reader. As such the meaning of the content is experienced through the meanings created by the visual design. We have considered how designers talk about magazine covers and also how scholarly approaches can help us to analyse these much more systematically. A look at the already massive and growing market in magazine templates seems to suggest that greater generic patterns in design will emerge in the future. In later chapters we go on to see that these basic design features can be found across different media platforms.

3 Changing Newspaper Designs for New Kinds of Markets

In this chapter we continue to look at fundamental design features that transfer across platforms, both in print and digital media. We look at the role of the image, typeface and colour, with particular attention given, in this instance, to composition. More specifically we focus on the way that in newspapers and news formats these visual tools can be used to communicate ideas and attitudes about titles designed for specific niche markets. It is not only text, or language itself, that communicates news messages and their meaning in a newspaper, nor even the photographs, but also the way it is presented or 'realised' through different visual tools. Award-winning newspaper designer Michael Crozier, who has worked on over 55 redesigns around the world, told us that journalists wrongly feel that design is nothing to do with them. Visual design, he expressed, is a fundamental part of the meaning of news content. Designers like Ron Reason told us that many newspapers now, in fact, think outwards from the visual design.

Most people are aware of different kinds of newspapers having a different 'look'. Readers even use the appearance of a tabloid newspaper to distinguish it from the more serious broadsheet newspaper, with the former being more associated with larger photographs and dramatic, large headlines. But fewer people will be aware of the subtleties or details of design choices that go into producing a newspaper.

These visual design choices form part of the meaning of the stories that the newspapers choose to cover, and carry information above and beyond that which is contained in the text and the pictures. Also, Crozier points out, the design must speak the visual language of the specific readership. As the newspaper industry has changed, as circulations have fallen off, especially for local news, as small ads have shifted online, and as readers themselves have changed their habits of information consumption, designers have been called upon to signal up new identities for titles that are struggling. Design becomes instrumental in helping newspapers to carry ideas and attitudes about news that allow them a place in the new communications landscape.

Javier Errea suggested that we still tend to talk about print media through older concepts associated with tabloid and broadsheet. But visual design has moved on. His designs, such as the French *Libération*, the Finnish *Aamulehti* and Swedish *Dagens Nyheter*, are all highly visual titles. Front pages will be dominated by a single photograph, which may be overlapped with text. Around this will sit smaller stories alongside other images, which have been given colour washes. Such titles represent a new era of design influenced by the look of web and mobile news platforms, and the reader and viewer expectations that go along with these. In this chapter we explore how designers harness typeface, colour, images and composition as a fundamental part of creating what news *is*.

We begin by looking at the influence of technology on page design. How newspapers look today needs to be considered within the historical context of how print and production technology has changed. We then look at design differences in three different genres of newspaper by gathering the observations of a number of designers interviewed at several newspapers. Two concrete examples of newspaper redesigns, done for different specific purposes, are analysed in more detail. The first is the major redesign of the *London Evening Standard* as it switched from a paid-for title to a newspaper distributed for free. We look at the design choices that were deployed in order for the publication to communicate to a specific target consumer group. The second is the free advertising-led local newspaper *The Harrow Times*, which was slightly modernised and changed to try to foreground the news and community aspect of the title as well as to strengthen visual links between the newspaper and its website. The final section looks at two cutting-edge designs from two award-winning designers that are setting new standards of newspaper design today.

Technology and newspaper design

The 1980s marked a huge change in newspaper design. Computer technology had created the potential for much more flexibility in design. But at the time the majority of staff employed in newspaper production were still working in the print room (typesetters and compositors) rather than on news desks. Much of the newspaper industry was still using the older traditional newspaper production methods. Even when computer technology was available to produce layouts, these were initially transferred to the printing press by so-called 'paste-up artists' using scalpels. Titles had huge numbers of staff. In London the *Daily Express* and *Sunday Express* had 6,800 employees in early 1986. By comparison, when the new full-colour daily paper *Today* was launched in the same year, one of the world's first papers to be produced fully electronically, its staff was only 600 (Crozier, 2010). But by present standards that number is also incredibly high.

In countries like the UK a conflict arose between news organisations and print unions. The shift to using the new technologies meant redundancies for a lot of people skilled in producing papers the old-fashioned way. But even prolonged strikes could not prevent the digital technologies from taking hold. For newspaper layout this point in time marked a revolution. The creative vision of editors, art directors and picture editors could much more directly and immediately be applied to a layout as they watched it being assembled on a computer screen right there in their editorial offices. Marc Reeves, publishing director at Trinity Mirror Midlands, who carried out a range of redesigns for Trinity Mirror regional titles, told us that this process wasn't in the hands of a compositor or 'paste-up' artist in the print room any more. Technology no longer limited newspaper design to fit into its parameters. As a result column widths, picture size and line spacing became more flexible and were now tweaked with greater precision.

Marc Reeves said that software like QuarkXpress and Adobe InDesign had matured by the late 1990s and become user-friendly enough to allow some editors to simply sit and play around with designs themselves. There was no longer a need for manually creating layout dummies to direct and contain the layout of each page into column widths. The software brought new speed and versatility. And sample copies can be quickly printed off to get a physical sense of the visual effect. Although, as Reeves explained, this process led sometimes to editors making changes simply because they could easily do so as opposed to these being part of a well-thought-out visual strategy.

The arrival of digital photography and editing software also brought massive changes to what could be achieved with page layout. These developments increased the speed at which images could be delivered and used as they could now be sent electronically, if necessary straight from the location. Images can now be viewed cheaply and quickly without the need to have negatives developed and printed. Editing software allowed the possibility of cut-out images, rapid collages and other forms of graphics, charts and compositional elements to be incorporated into designs much more creatively. We will see below one particular example of a more magazine-style, visually creative newspaper.

From the 1990s onwards more and more emphasis is placed on how newspapers look and how this affects their sales – their success or otherwise. Although Marc Reeves did suggest that there have been waves of redesigns since the end of the 1990s and particularly in the early years of the 21st century, which were management-led and oriented to reviving titles with flagging circulations and dwindling advertising that were not clearly founded on market research and which proved largely unsuccessful. For example, the *Liverpool Post* was redesigned for a more upmarket reader in 2003 (Machin and Niblock, 2008). Market research had profiled a more professional readership, which designers needed to address. One problem is that such redesigns can alienate established readers without considering that the desired younger professional group is less likely to take on a newspaper-buying habit. Marc suggested that in his own experience of managing restructuring at Trinity Mirror titles, redesigns could sometimes be equated with the rearranging of deckchairs on sinking ships. He said that years of complacency in terms of advertising revenue, circulations and the arrival of the web could not so easily be addressed by a simple redesign. However, as we see in this chapter, some redesigns can be part of successful relaunches, as in the case of the *London Evening Standard*, which shifted to a free version in 2012. In such cases the redesign helps in clarifying the identity and feel of the content the paper is providing and improves the navigation through the publication by establishing visual pathways for the reader to follow.

Also important in the changing look of newspapers was that full-colour printing became universally available and affordable in the 1990s (Conboy, 2014). Aside from the emergence of online news platforms, which will be dealt with in more detail in a separate chapter, this was the latest technological change affecting the look of today's newspapers.

It may be true that most readers are barely aware of the typefaces, colours and column grids used. But Michael Crozier emphasises that the newer kind of newspaper design, which was pioneered partly in the UK by his newspaper at the time, *The Independent*, which won awards for its innovative use of graphics, had to have a sophisticated sense of how these elements communicate. There are examples of local newspapers that have been brought back from the brink of financial disaster by an overhaul of their appearance. But Crozier emphasises that as technology became cheap and more people were able to use it, designs were done quickly and in-house, often without a clear understanding of colour or fonts.

Although, as we see in this chapter, redesigns can be done for a range of reasons, including refreshing a title, market repositioning, harmonising a group of regional titles to allow easy syndication of content and also as a way to create multi-platform brands. This process has become fast, convenient and economically viable. It can be done instinctively, as opposed to being based on market research, and does not even always have to involve experienced designers. It is with this context in mind that we now look at some hypothetical and actual newspaper designs.

The language of newspaper design

In this section our aim is to examine some of the core principles of the language of newspaper design. Before presenting some actual examples of design choices in practice we first draw on our interviews to analyse how designers can harness fonts, colours, borders, space, positioning, images and a range of other visual tools to communicate ideas, attitudes and values about, not only the newspaper, but also about the meaning of specific news stories. For that purpose we have devised three mock newspapers, based on generic newspaper types: the broadsheet, the tabloid and a relatively new type of newspaper, which we have come to refer to as 'Metro' style, the free London paper *Metro* being one of the first newspapers of this type to emerge. The dummy layouts are based on the accounts of our interviewees, particularly Michael Crozier, who has redesigned across genres for over 55 titles in 14 countries. In each case we talk through the different design features in turn. They have been created using identical page sizes, even though the three styles of paper may use different page formats, and size certainly was traditionally one of the main distinguishing features between the look of a broadsheet and that of a tabloid. There is much less differentiation in sizes between the different paper types nowadays, and for ease of comparison we have therefore disregarded size.

The broadsheet and visual composition

In Figure 3.1 we can see the three different newspaper designs. Even if the text were exactly the same on each, this would be experienced very differently because of the distinctive kinds of visual realisation.

Figure 3.1   Three generic newspaper designs (from left to right: broadsheet, 'Metro' style and tabloid), with underlying column grids displayed

Mastheads

The masthead of the broadsheet is set in Goudy Text MT Regular. Such fonts, found seldom in other places, point to history and tradition. Michael Crozier, who had redesigned a number of broadsheets, was not keen on traditional fonts based on very early typefaces, feeling that current readers would experience them as dated. This mock masthead is probably most reminiscent of *The Daily Telegraph* in the UK, *Le Monde* in France or *Frankfurter Allgemeine Zeitung* in Germany. Reader familiarity across many decades, Crozier says, makes such papers reluctant to change fonts, particularly when these titles often tend to have a more established and older readership. Marc Reeves explained to us that many newspaper redesigns had resulted in alienating established readers while not necessarily attracting new ones.

The Masthead on the 'Metro' style newspaper is very different. It is set in Georgia Bold, which is a simple serif font that is much less traditional. The overall letter height has been compressed to 91% to make it appear less 'lofty' and slightly more grounded. This font is also much lighter than might be found on some more traditional titles that seek to be perceived in the traditional newspaper role of 'reliable informer'. It is a font whose roundness suggests something organic and feminine. Designers we spoke with said it was warm and friendly. It suggests a shift away from the traditional and authoritative to something more evenly gendered and gentle.

Importantly, the two words that form the masthead have been positioned more dynamically rather than just using them on one single line. This breaks up the masthead and makes it instantly look more lively and less formal.

In the case of the tabloid we find Sans Serif Eurostile LT Std typeface in its Bold Oblique version. Being set in italics gives it a sense of energy as it leans obliquely to the right. The weight of the font suggests much more certainty and stability of viewpoint. We also find a sense of masculinity and technicality through the angularity of the font. The masthead itself is not separated from the contents but appears as one of the elements of the busy design.

Date strap

Designers told us that this was an important part of the way that newspapers create their identities. And indeed the design of the date strap is very differently approached in our three covers. The broadsheet uses a bar of space with two hairline horizontal lines, which suggest elegance and precision – values that Lee Bearton, Art Director News of the *Evening Standard*, suggested would be less attractive values to a younger professional market. A further horizontal line in the same weight (0.25pt) is used further down the page to separate stories. The use of such lines to divide up the page can calm the page and provides contrast to the long, thin vertical text columns, which give the page a dense feel.

On the 'Metro' style cover the date strap tends to form a whole separate section. In this case it is delineated by the date strap at the bottom and a bar at the top with the website URL. The cut-out image to the right is more reminiscent of a magazine supplement cover device. Significantly this design carries lots of space, partly important in creating a sense of expansiveness and ease of access. We find overlapping used here as the image lies over the space of the bar at the top and the finer one below. While tabloids use much more energetic overlapping, this cover is more measured in its approach. The cut-out successfully creates visual interest.

The masthead on tabloids is often in a slightly bigger red block that also contains the date strap. As the tabloid market is particularly competitive and the target readership is from a less affluent demographic than is the case with broadsheets, the price is often highlighted separately. It appears in an elliptical price tag. Playing with setting contrasting shapes such as circles and squares and contrasting colours against each other is a typical tabloid design strategy. The tabloid masthead is therefore usefully employed to generate a feel of energy and directness.

Headlines and fonts

The headlines of the broadsheet are all set in Arno Pro Semibold Display. Although released in 2007 this font has a traditional appearance reminiscent of 15th- and 16th-century early humanistic typefaces. It is used for its elegance, with its longer descenders combined with lower x-height, which designers often feel points to a little sense of antiquity and feels suitable for books that deal with history. This very much chimes with what Conboy (2014) has written on the association of news with old Enlightenment values. The font overall is also compact and traditional, with serifs giving a sense of unity and certainty. Again Michael Crozier did not feel these were now suitable fonts to use in newspaper design exactly for this reason. Later in the chapter we see how some contemporary designs seek to communicate quite the opposite meaning.

On the 'Metro' style cover there is more variation in the headline design than on the conventional broadsheet. Lee Bearton told us that these 'Metro' style titles tend to have three modern fonts, which are used systematically to create balance and links across the page. The main headline is set in Romain BP Headline Black at 120pt size with 105pt leading, which makes the lines sit close together. This is a modern typeface with very big thick/thin contrast and vertical stress (i.e. the thin bits in the O, for example, are directly on top of each other rather than being diagonally positioned as is the case in Oldstyle fonts). This font would not look out of place in a contemporary lifestyle magazine or on a perfume advertisement. The fonts overall will be modern and are used with slightly greater spacing between lines and wrapped in white space.

On the tabloid the headline placing is much more flexible yet tends to take up the majority of space on the cover and is often designed around the main picture. So the large blue background area could in this case actually be an image. And often headlines will share the same space as the image, blending meaning. The wording fuses with the photograph, which in the case of tabloids can often be very misleading (Conboy, 2006). The main headline uses a font aptly named Impact. On tabloids headlines on one page can use a variety of fonts to create a sense of variety and liveliness in contrast to the single font of a formal title.

Page structure

The column and page structure of the three covers is also fundamentally different. For the broadsheet we find most of the page divided into five vertical columns, which in relation to its width gives fairly narrow text columns. Older newspapers often used more columns, which made the page appear very dense, suggesting a page that required time to get through. We see fewer columns on the 'Metro' newspaper, where there is great need to bring a sense of ease of reading. Longer line measures facilitate reading for readers on moving trains as the eye doesn't have to jump from the end of one line to the beginning of the next quite as frequently. On the tabloid we only find one text column in this example. The tabloid cover is more about communicating the attitude of the newspaper as forthright and confident, and certainly does not want to give the impression that stories will require extensive reading.

One thing that designers talk about as key for designing newspapers is the grid. Bearton of the *Evening Standard* spoke extensively on the use of the grid in a redesign to create a different sense of space and a consistent pace throughout the newspaper. Grids are an important part of the page templates that exist, so that newspapers don't have to be designed from scratch every day. They provide an underlying structure for the different page elements such as pictures, headlines, text columns etc. to fit into. Different designers use varying complexities of horizontal and vertical lines to divide up the page into a grid. But most commonly what is referred to as the grid is a set of vertical lines that divides up the page into equal strips of space (columns) with a set amount of gap between them, known as the gutter.

Grids shape the use of spacing and relative positioning. Often the underlying grid of the page is more complex than is apparent to the eye. We can see in the example of the broadsheet that the images are placed overlapping several columns but always obeying their boundaries. The Metro-style cover uses more gridlines but always overlaps these in terms of width of text columns, which are then given lots of white padding to create space. While the very even distribution of text columns on the broadsheet results in a very measured feel, the Metro front page places the two cover stories in this example across four columns and three columns respectively. This gives it an off-beat feel, much like a syncopated rhythm would in a piece of music. Having more columns also creates more flexibility. And with the free commuter titles, as Lee Bearton told us, there is a need to have variety across subsequent covers in order to maintain interest. The tabloid uses a larger number of narrower grid columns. This facilitates the placing of lots of different sizes of boxes and information so that different columns can be used and overlapped. This is part of creating energy and allowing a variety of shapes, forms and sizes to be playfully arranged against each other.

One further important unique characteristic in the Metro newspaper is that there is generally no separate list of contents. The various signposts around the page are used in its place. The front page strongly fulfils the function of being an advertisement for the inside pages of the newspaper. The newspaper cover must itself provide incentive for commuters to pick it up. Once they have done so, they will then flick through. Matt Phare spoke of the decision on the free commuter magazine *ShortList* to carry only a celebrity on the cover with no other indication of specific contents.

Framing and colour bars

These are also important parts of the different page layout approaches, signifying reading experiences, ideas and attitudes. Michael Crozier told us that he himself had taken training in the use of colour at the Poynter Institute in Florida, learning principles he has since utilised on newspapers around the world. In the case of the Metro-style paper colour has become very important and has led to these titles having a much more magazine-type look, which itself is indicative of a shift away from hard news and information to lifestyle interest and entertainment. Colour-filled boxes and frames are used to create visual focus and to break up the page. The colour schemes are also now brighter than in the reds and browns associated with more serious current affairs magazines. Colour is also used in elements across the page to create rhyming – so a yellow in one of the bars will also be used in some text lower on the page or on a text box.

For the tabloid there is a lot of flexibility regarding colour, although it is used differently. Predominating colours are usually red, black and bright yellow, which is used for contrasts and to create brightness. A larger colour palette can signify fun and playfulness in contrast to the more moderate and reserved moods indicated by a more restricted palette.

As we see later in the chapter, there has been a tendency to move away from colour bars and frames in order to move to a more 'open' sense of news.

Pictures

It is the case, as we show in concrete examples shortly, that newspapers now tend to broadly use images much more and in different ways than they did even five years ago. But there remain some key differences. On the broadsheet cover there are two images. One is a larger image for the top news story in the top half of the page and above the fold. These can be quite literal, for example, showing two politicians talking. But even in more traditional broadsheets it is now common to find more informal cut-out images and other kinds of more inventive displays.

On the Metro front page it is not unusual to have a large dominant picture taking up the majority of space. The headline may then overlap much of the image, which has been cropped and chosen precisely for this purpose. It may also be more symbolic than literal and documentary. For example, a large public event will be represented by one person shot in close-up to show their facial expression and thereby communicate a mood, rather than showing a wider-angle view and just documenting the large scale of the event. The image may also offer a 'creative' and involved point of view. So rather than just looking onto a scene the viewer looks over the shoulder of a participant, or looks up from a low angle as if somehow implicated in the ongoing events. All this is related to new ways of signalling the relationship between the newspaper and the reader.

The banner across the top can also contain a picture. It can be a panoramic picture across the width of the page with text inset, or as in this case a coloured box containing a picture and a headline. This functions very much like a signpost, indicating that the title contains some fun, lifestyle content and entertainment.

What is also often characteristic of the images carried by these more stylised newspapers is that they themselves are used as part of the design as opposed to the more traditional function of bearing witness. All the newspaper designers we interviewed mentioned that editors now had to think in a whole new way about the use of images as part of layouts. The front cover of the *The Independent* shown in the Introduction is one example of how Crozier pioneered this technique. Such compositions are now often seen across Metro-style newspaper pages.

On the tabloid much creativity goes into working with cover pictures. Images can often form part of collages, appear in differently shaped and framed boxes, and very often with cut-outs. Pictures can also be feathered at the edges so they appear to 'bleed' onto the background colour of the text box. All this signifies energy and reduced formality.

The black and the grey box at the top would be used to carry an image, with the headlines overlaid over the top. The two green boxes would be used to carry mugshots of people. The emphasis here will be on individual persons rather than processes and events.

Redesigns 1: The *London Evening Standard*

The *Evening Standard* was redesigned in 2009. The redesign was the work of art directors Nick Cave, Lee Bearton and typography consultant Paul Barnes. Editor Geordie Greig wanted to move away from the older informer style, which was very dense. As Bearton said to us: 'If you read this older version of the *Standard*, then you really wanted to read it.' Bearton also said that there was a strong sense that the title had lost its connection with London. It had been in decline for many years. At the Society of Editors conference in 2009 Greig announced that the 180-year-old *Standard* would not have survived another year had drastic measures not been taken. Circulations had been declining about 10% a year for ten years. In an interview Simon Fox, the new head of Trinity Mirror, in 2013 pointed to the huge problems facing local newspapers, with falling readerships and a younger generation not sharing the former culture of regular newspaper buying. The world had changed. People under 28 had simply stopped reading newspapers. Free titles could be picked up at tube stations, or those discarded on the seats by other commuters could be taken. There were two, *Londonlite* and the *London Paper*, in the evening and one, the *Metro*, in the morning. This created a very crowded market place for London-wide local papers and with three free papers supplying London news a paid-for title was always going to struggle to compete. Moreover the *Standard* belonged to an old era where newspapers saw themselves in a traditional role of informer. Earlier in 2009 the title had been taken over by Russian businessman Alexander Lebedev, and had previously been owned by the *Daily Mail* and General Trust. In these former years many readers had associated the newspaper with the conservative *Mail*, and it had shared the editor in chief with this publication.

On its launch the new *Standard* included some more upmarket commentary such as a satirical piece by author Tom Wolfe. Greig had previously run the magazine *Tatler*, and the aim was to shift the paper away from drier reporting to more entertainment and lifestyle. But Bearton stressed that maintaining a sense that the *Standard* was a quality informer providing reliable, well-researched news was also a prime consideration during the redesign. The *Standard* switched from being a paid-for paper with a 50p cover price to a 'quality-free', immediately tripling its distribution to 600,000 copies a day. It also transformed its whole economic model by reducing the price of distribution from 30p a copy to only 4p. Part of this was the switch from individual sellers to mass placement of copies at tube stations. The title was selling about 700 copies a day at Holborn tube station, which grew to 10,000 being given out free. Other savings were made through cutting some editions to only have one later edition and focusing distribution on key areas inside London's Zone 2. And newsagents were now paying to get the title in to attract customers as opposed to taking a cut of the sales price. There were also job losses as subbing was outsourced to the Press Association. While rebrands are often delivered to the public, Marc Reeves pointed out, as a new and exciting face to their newspaper, they are more often part of quite cynical overall restructures where titles across a region are given the same look to allow easy syndication of content, resulting in some local closures and certainly in huge staffing reductions. But given the massive declines in circulations of local newspapers, it is hard to see other business alternatives.

When we spoke to Lee Bearton he said that the remit from the editor at the time was mainly to aim to attract a specific group of professional wealthier readers. This group would be travelling on the tube at the time the edition would come out. Importantly, readers under the age of 28 were of particular interest to the paper from a commercial point of view. The paper also had to address them as Londoners. Greig had felt that the title had lost some of its role of addressing the community. Bearton said the new design also needed to work for commuting. With average tube journeys being 20 minutes long, the paper needed to feel like it could be picked up and engaged with in this time period. This was particularly important for advertisers who wanted assurance that each reader would go through an entire edition.

So the redesign had a lot of expectations to live up to, and the first change in the design was an alteration of the grid (Figure 3.2). As we noted in the analysis earlier in the chapter, this is something that might go unseen by the viewer but which has a huge influence on the visual appearance of the page. The change in the grid was one important way a look of spaciousness was created. When we asked about the main elements of the redesign it was the new grid that Bearton wanted to talk about first. This had been reduced to use fewer and wider columns. On all the newer *Standard* covers we see the wider columns, always with space allowed above and below. Line spacing was also increased and more white space was used generally throughout. This created a 'lite' look but also aided reading standing up and when in motion. These are precisely the kinds of devices we pointed to for the Metro-type newspaper in the earlier section.

Figure 3.2 The *Evening Standard*, 2008 and after the rebrand in 2013

But for the most part attracting these younger readers meant a design that pointed to greater stylisation and which clearly indicated entertaining content, tit-bits and lifestyle as opposed to feeling like the old formal informer. This stylisation was achieved through a switch to more modern fonts and the use of only three, which were Publico, Amplitude and Stag. Bearton said that the earlier version had used many more different fonts across the pages, which gave a less tidy look, and that the new fonts had a much more modern, spacious feel. They combine curvature and angularity but also create space by combining slimmer and wider uprights and horizontal lines.

Importantly these three fonts are used across the composition to create links between elements. They allow these units to 'rhyme'. This could also be interpreted as part of the breaking down of the barriers between different genres of contents. It is not so much that this is about tabloidisation but simply that all contents are designed to look like they all offer a similarly easy reading experience.

Stylisation and ease of reading, Bearton said, have also been achieved through the use of borders and framing. The masthead has been given much greater room to breathe and is framed alongside an entertainment teaser. The colours of the frames also play an important role in creating a magazine-influenced look. The *Standard* had been using its trademark blue at the top of the page. But the new design uses a blue, red and orange colour scheme. The orange especially, a sunny colour, brings a lightness characteristic not of the darker, more traditional news colours, but more of a magazine. The corporate blue, a colour hue often associated with coolness and the rational as opposed to the more emotional and sensuous reds, forms the header while the orange forms the border, which contains the contents below the masthead. The increase of colour palette from black and white to one colour, blue, to the use of three colours can also have another semiotic effect. More limited colour palettes can suggest restraint and measure, whereas more expansive colour palettes can suggest fun, liveliness or garishness. These three colours – the colder blue, more emotional red and bright orange – with their contrasting nature do suggest more liveliness and energy. But importantly these colours are used moderately. A tabloid style may use big splashes of colour. Here they are used in key places to soften the page and to create textual links gently and tastefully.

But while images have become much more dominant it is important that we do not find the buzzing overlap we might expect from a highly tabloid newspaper or magazine. Bearton emphasised the need for measure and to indicate the 'quality news' aspect of the title. And clearly the newspaper design uses this to point to an increased visual interest as opposed to the lively raucousness of the tabloid. Overlapping will be reserved more for lifestyle and entertainment, compared to tabloid newspapers where it is used throughout.

Redesign 2: The local advertiser

In this section we look at some less sweeping, but nevertheless significant, changes to a raft of free advertising news-sheets from around the Greater London area in the UK. What the interviews for this book have made clear is that design operates at vastly different levels of staffing and costs across different parts of the industry. And much of this is done off-the-cuff by non-specialists. In this case the design changes were all carried out by editor in chief of the titles, Rachel Sharp, who had worked as an editor before for many years and was brought in to address dwindling advertising and faltering public engagement, which is precisely what the redesigns, she felt, helped to do. Sharp ran and developed five Newsquest titles from 2007: *Harrow Times*; *Edgeware and Mill Hill Times*; *Barnet and Potters Bar Times*; *Hillingdon Times* and the

Hendon Times. What was clear at this time was that with online competition for free ads and also falling interest in local print news there was a need to modernise the look of the titles and also to help foster an online presence.

Sharp had received no design training and there was no budget to bring in a team. Rather, being unhappy with the look of the titles, she began to look online at the way other titles had been redesigned to create a tidier and more contemporary look.

Here we look at a few of the key changes that she made, which were part of a process of turning the publications around and massively increasing the number of visitors to the newspaper websites, which had been one of the remits for her job. Sharp was quick to see that the print version needed more accessibility, signposting and design elements that would lead people to want to see more. She was clear that readers now expected a different standard of visual experience from newspapers.

One of the big problems of the design was that space was not being well used or thought through. There was simply not enough editorial space, and the little editorial content there was, was getting lost among the advertisements. One problem with such local titles is that there are massive constraints on space and compositional possibilities created by the priority of advertising content.

Sharp needed to work with the space she had and make better use of it. She changed all of the titles to being web-first. So they needed a multi-platform look. She decided to put stories online upfront, and the best then appeared in the print version. Also she decided to put all readers' letters online, with some in print. She put links to online interviews on the print version to expand stories. And she also wanted to further localise the content of all the papers as many were running the same stories. So the print copies became a leader for the online versions. But she also needed to create some visual signposts that heralded a more contemporary newspaper-reading experience.

We can see a few of these in the two front covers in Figure 3.3. First, the newer designs have much more space, balance and symmetry. Sharp said that a cluttered look simply failed to tally with contemporary reader expectations. Through moving the advertisements to the bottom of the page, the editorial content can now spread out across the entire width of the page. Metaphorically this gives the material room to breathe. Sharp also changed the position of the date. It has been placed in a blue box with lots of empty space. This involved a battle with advertisers who wanted the coveted 'bookend' positions. But Rachel knew she needed to re-engage readers, and as readers and web hits increased dramatically

Figure 3.3   Harrow Times, before and after the redesign

the advertisers too were pleased. The masthead has also been reduced in size and moved down the page slightly. Space has been created between the words 'Harrow' and 'Times', connoting a title where there is room to breathe and space to contemplate.

Secondly, wider columns have been used. This has been common in redesigns and communicates that there is not too much dense reading. Rachel also moved away from text justified on both left and right to a ragged right edge. Text that is justified on both sides is generally used to communicate greater formality and seriousness as it appears controlled and disciplined. Leaving it ragged on one side appears more informal and natural. We find a more careful use of the alignment of elements. Designers we interviewed point to the importance of alignment to create a sense of peace and order on the page. On the older version we find that the headline sits awkwardly with the alignment of the columns below, and different sizes of images have been used. On the new version we find the single column at the left and then the rest aligned under the masthead.

A story bar at the left was introduced. It is important to have these snippets or teasers, and with increasing dominance of online news outlets, readers are very much used to navigating to content via teasers. One of the problems with advertisement titles is that they very easily suggest to readers that they have little editorial content. Comparing the two covers, we immediately get a sense that the new version has more content and more substance than the older version. The story bar has also been used to heighten the sense of spaciousness. Sharp said that older designs may have wanted to put more in here, but she resisted the temptation. It was not that design was to have priority over content but that she needed to find visual ways to deliver editorial to readers. Changes in content and labelling, but also visual changes, helped to do so.

Rachel also realised that the use of colour was now completely different on the modern newspaper. While it was not possible to increase the number of colours for the *Harrow Times* it was possible nevertheless to use the blue to create rhyming across the page. So the blue was re-employed for the text headings down the left-hand side. Immediately this links with the bar beneath the masthead and the date box to help give the page a sense of structure and coherence. Overall colour and colour bars have been used throughout the newspaper to create links and rhyming.

In other places text boxes were coloured with pale blue washes. While saturated colour can suggest emotional warmth or intensity, dilute colours can point to emotional moderation and gentleness. Utility bills often use these colours to reduce their impact. Of course, more dilute colours would also be impractical as they might interfere with the readability of any text placed inside such a box.

As with the *Evening Standard*, Sharp also made changes in the use of fonts. More modern sans serif fonts were used for straplines, bylines and captions. And she cut the number of fonts, again to reduce the sense of clutter.

One more important design decision involved the use of photographs. First of all there was a decision to use images throughout that show actual people in ways that personalise them, preferably showing them reacting, as opposed to images of settings or posed groups and officials. As we saw in the chapter on photojournalism, it is these posed group images – children standing in front of a closing local school with their thumbs down – that form the clichés of the local press. Sharp was fully aware of this. We can see this on the front page. The older version shows a setting with an inset mugshot. The newer version personalises the protagonists as it avoids the more static posed shot. This is striking on the Community Calendar pages (Figure 3.4). As well as careful use of colour bars to give the page form, the image is much more dynamic in contrast to the posed and clichéd local event shot.

The presentation of photos is as important as the typographic design and structure of the written content. Sharp said that there was a tendency on local newspapers to carry fairly closely cropped images. Typical of these are the pictures of the people on the older Community Calendar pages. On the new version the framing of the picture deliberately gives more room to the person. Not only does this add to the

Figure 3.4 Harrow Times: use of images and colour on Community Calendar pages

sense of spaciousness on the page the redesign is aiming for, it also helps to give a greater sense of individualisation to the protagonist. It adds a greater sense of elegance to images and retains more of the skill of the photographer in creating a pleasing composition in the picture. It used to be a common complaint of photographers that once their pictures were put into a newspaper layout, they would be cropped to within an inch of their life and reduced to a very literal rendering of the subject with no regard to what the space around the subject added to its meaning. This newer image, Sharp says, is more typical of contemporary use where greater respect is given to the original framing of the shot. This helps in communicating emotion and energy.

Aside from the different picture treatment, the fonts and text spacing and justification on the Community Calendar pages have changed too. Local events have been removed and replaced with an invitation to go online to see these. This was part of a raft of decisions that led to a successful increase in web traffic. And only a sample of readers' letters were printed, with the promise that all received would be published online.

In sum Rachel Sharp's successful redesign of the paper abandons cramped, dense pages, making the paper appear less demanding and reading it simply a more pleasant experience. While this means loss of quantity of content, this always comes with the promise of additional information online. Colour bars create rhyming across the page and make the look of the paper more pleasing to the eye, as do the more modern fonts, the increased use of white space, careful page positioning and alignment, and the use of more contemporary-looking photographs instead of the dull standard local newspaper picture. While some of these design strategies may not be suitable for all newspapers, they have worked for decluttering local free-sheets.

The award-winning designs

In this next section we look at two contemporary and cutting-edge designs by award-winning international designers. First is the work of Javier Errea, a Spanish designer, who has done redesigns internationally for *Libération* in France and Sweden's *Dagens Nyheter* along with newspapers in South America and New Zealand. Errea has a journalism degree and formerly worked as a reporter and editor. Second we look at a redesign example from Ron Reason, a design consultant based in Chicago, USA. He has redesigned publications including *Advertising Age*, *The Dallas Morning News*, *Orlando Sentinel*, *Boston Herald*, *Emirates* (Dubai) *Evening Post*, *The Standard of Nairobi*, *Kenya* and many others, and worked in Brazil and India. He is involved in the Poynter Institute, where he has served as Director of Visual Journalism. As with Javier Errea, he originally trained as a journalist but found himself drawn to editing and design. He understood the communicative power of the visual journalist.

Aamulehti, Finland

For Javier Errea this was a particularly interesting project. For over 100 years until the spring of 2014 *Aamulehti* had been what he called a standard-format newspaper, with a broadsheet-type identity. The redesign was part of a complete overhaul of the title, including the editorial team and type of contents. The newspaper was to switch to a more tabloid style and have two types of content with both professional journalism, providing content with a strongly informative identity, and local public-driven content, including short stories, commentaries, complaints, etc. The aim was to create a newspaper that was clearly in dialogue with its readers. Also the redesign had another aim, which follows a more international pattern. *Aamulehti* was the leading title of a group of local and regional titles. The redesign was to facilitate easy sharing of pages and contents across the different papers (Figure 3.5).

Javier said that the old version of the design was very masculine. He saw it as hard and distant. This was partly down to the choice of font, mainly Flama and Morgan Avec, but also to its ordered appearance. The older version used more borders and hierarchies of headings. It was a smart-looking design in the direction of the Metro-style look with image cut-outs, but appears text-heavy and with short introductions to many stories appearing on the front page.

Javier said that the challenge for this redesign was to adopt a tabloid format but maintain a serious feel. In terms of content one innovation has been to include public commentaries on the front page. In terms of visual design the aim was to lose some of the hardness and to make it more accessible, more optimistic and, importantly, more feminine and delicate. So the first step was to get rid of lines, which dominate the older version. New typefaces were brought in – Metric for information and Prumo for softer material. Metric is a typeface constructed from geometric shapes and connotes order in a simple and direct way. It also offers combinations of sharp angles and soft curves, as can be seen in the headline. For Javier it was a fresh and gentle typeface. We can also see on the cover that the headline is lower case and not particularly bold. But it is clearly a simple geometric font. The letter 't' has complete symmetry, for example. The 'o' is close to being a simple circle. All these kinds of devices help to communicate ideas of simplicity, ease and accessibility.

A particular issue thrown up by the font choice for this paper is a quirk of some of the Scandinavian languages. Their alphabets contain

Figure 3.5 Aamulehti, front covers

the letters ä, ö and ü. Some fonts can make this appear very square, which needed to be avoided in making the design appear more delicate.

In terms of page structure the design makes use of a complex grid based on 30 columns. The advertising structure sits across five columns, which matches other newspapers in the group to facilitate selling of ad space across several titles simultaneously. But Javier said that the 30-column format (with the five ad columns taking up six grid columns each to make 30 in total) was perfect for controlling distances between elements and also for creating space, important to bring in the gentleness and serenity they were looking for. We can see from the redesign, that, as in the *London Evening Standard* example above, the amount of white space created is striking. Along with the simple fonts this becomes almost meditative. While there has been a decrease in the use of borders for segregation there has been an increase in the use of space for separation. The masthead is allowed to sit in luxurious amounts of space, as is the headline. But the higher number of columns used, along with the teasers at the bottom of the design, maintain the sense that the title is still information-rich. On the inside pages we find eight narrow columns of text. They appear accessible yet at the same time suggest quantity of information. This is a different approach from the Metro-style *Evening Standard*, where all contents must appear as readable almost at a glance. As Javier Errea said, the task here is to combine features of accessible tabloids with the feel of the traditional informer.

Colour has also been changed in the redesign. On the old design colours such as the orange were used well for linking elements on the page and for communicating hierarchies. But the new design has moved away from this model. A cheerful green box predominates below the masthead containing the sports headline and a bright yellow highlight in the photograph. Green is used for sports throughout. There is a clear emphasis on bright, vibrant saturated colours. These work well alongside the space and geometric fonts. The colours are used as accents. Regulation and excessive rhyming is avoided.

Javier said that a focus on photography and picture editing are key aspects of the new *Aamulehti*. Of course images are typically more important in tabloid formats. But the difference here is that they must be good-quality, striking images. In the chapter on photojournalism we looked at the kinds of photographers who specialise in making more striking, stylised images that appear to create a particular viewpoint on a situation rather than documenting it literally. We see this on the main photograph on the new design. We are given the perspective of the men standing on the steps with the men in uniform facing us. Such images engage the reader and create interest in the page. But they also communicate, as the photojournalists told us, a particular set of ideas about a particular type of viewing and viewer. These images provide a more dynamic placement of vantage point in contrast to the former literal, bearing witness-type images. This particular photograph actually positions the viewer right inside the unfolding event and creates a sense of participation in the depicted situation. The primary image on each double page will also usually cut across the fold. This is part of avoiding symmetric structures. And across pages rhythmic patterns are avoided. Again this is about communicating an attitude. The older title was regulated, hard and about certainties. The redesign is about engagement, thoughtfulness but also delicacy, appealing for both men and women's participation and contributions. This is a very different set of ideas and attitudes regarding news than the older model of the authoritative informer.

Capital Ideas, Chicago

Ron Reason is an internationally known American designer who has worked across genres on national and local newspapers in the US and worldwide. He told us that he particularly works in areas where titles discover they have the need to speak more clearly to niche markets. He spoke particularly for the need not to underestimate the role of advertising in redesigns. Before taking a job he speaks with business and marketing people to understand the kind of reader the design needs to attract. But importantly he wants to understand the title journalistically. After he personally has assessed four editions of the title in terms of design, accessibility and coherence, he asks the editor what they think is wrong with the look of the newspaper, how the readership has changed and how the design should change to keep up with them. He always tries to establish what would make him engage with these stories even though he may not be the target reader. Ron has a journalism degree himself but has worked in design for many years.

Here we look at one example of Ron's work on the redesign of the University of Chicago's business research magazine, *Capital Ideas*. Overall he had felt that the old design had insufficient editorial focus. There was no coherent voice. He said that often his redesigns mean bringing in sharply focused templates across titles, but also leaving room for creativity. And importantly it had been felt that the design should signpost the more serious journalistic nature of the content. So in one sense the design needed to signal up a more authoritative identity. He also felt that there was insufficient navigation in the magazine and that throughout it needed to feel much cleaner.

The old cover and the redesign are shown in Figures 3.6 and 3.7. The old covers used generic stock artwork, often with Photoshop effects, but had nothing to do with the content inside the magazine. And, Reason said, there was no active headline. The appearance was more of a promotional brochure than of editorial and journalism. On the new cover the image is clearly connected to the headline but also plays a symbolic role. An older type, more literal image would show a scene from a demonstration. Here the image more playfully hints at the idea of the demonstration (Figure 3.7), while remaining upbeat with high levels of brightness in the upper centre of the image and the colour coordination of red, blue and yellow. Red is used throughout for fonts, such as the contents bar at the bottom.

On the redesign we find more white space, but also text is more condensed, giving a sense of quantity of information and content. This contrasts to the older pages, which in fact appear light on content. There is much space, but rather than helping content it simply brings the impression of there being little substance on each page, which is not good for a title that seeks to signpost its informative nature. The uses of borders are also problematic. The narrow border between the title and the body of the text is poorly used. Borders can be used to group separate

Figure 3.6   Capital Ideas: the old look of the front cover

Figure 3.7   Capital Ideas: the new look

contents. And they can do this to different degrees. Thicker borders can create greater barriers between contents, whereas thin or dotted borders appear much more permeable and reduce segregation. In this case why is the headline segregated from the contents? In the newer version we see much more integration of contents, although here empty space is used to separate rather than to segregate. The headline, placed at the bottom, helps to bring the page alive. It is right-justified, which adds to a sense of informality. Headlines themselves have become more clearly informative. In the old version it was not easy to guess what the items would be about. We see the new clarity in 'What Occupy Wall Street should have said' (Figure 3.8) and 'Financial reform: What's been done and what remains?' (Figure 3.9). Ron Reason stressed that his experience as a journalist drew him to thinking about how headlines would be speaking to readers in general, but in each case how they reflected the broader ideas and attitudes the publication wished to convey.

Reason himself has talked about the different effects of the presentation of headlines, although he emphasises that most important is that this stays in line with the identity of the title. But he illustrates the effect

Figure 3.8   Capital Ideas: new-look double-page spread

Figure 3.9   Capital Ideas: another spread from the magazine's new look

of this on one page of *Capital Ideas* magazine (Figure 3.10). In the first iteration of the design we see the same font size used throughout the headline, with a right-justified alignment. This is far less formal than a left-justified text. The second example, which was chosen by the magazine, experiments with different font sizes. The last is much more playful, and while perfect for bringing life to pages, was not considered right for this magazine, with its interest in communicating a greater sense of authority.

The fonts used on the older pages have a higher degree of curvature compared to the angularity of the very rational new sans serif font, which creates a sense of modernity. Immediately these qualities point to something more technical and up to date. Headlines also tend to use a more horizontally spread font, suggesting stability. But we also find slim, tall and condensed fonts for subheadings, as in 'How to fix the global financial system'. Again these are modern and sophisticated. But these condensed typefaces, Reason explained, were also important for communicating depth of content. They may well be avoided in contexts such as the Metro-style newspaper where there is need to point to

Figure 3.10   Capital Ideas: three different design ideas for an opening page

ease of reading and lightness. Of course, however, these denser sections of text will be combined with white space and infographics. As Javier Errea, designer of *Dagens Nyheter*, told us, these can be characterised as two kinds of rhythms of reading, the more staggered and the more condensed.

In *Capital Ideas* a new careful and deliberate use of colour has been introduced. It is unclear how colour was used in the older versions (Figure 3.11), but in the new version one vibrant, bright colour is used to different degrees of saturation, for borders, box fills, headlines and drop caps across the page. This leads to greater stylisation and helps to create a sense of order and regulation that may not work for a different type of publication. But here the title seeks to foreground rigour, precision and quality reporting.

Conclusion

In this chapter we have seen how multimodality draws our attention to the changing nature of design in print media. The use of visual elements and composition has become more sophisticated, to signal ideas and to point to new kinds of attitudes of newspapers. They seek to disassociate themselves from their old image as authoritative informers, which readers have grown to turn away from. Instead they aim to be perceived to be more airy, entertainment-related publications, guiding readers through careful use of page rhyming, signposting and positioning and

Figure 3.11   Capital Ideas: a marked-up double-page design

overall simplification of details such as fonts and alignment. This is not just changing the look of newspapers but is part of news having to seek out a new identity for itself with which it can go to the public. News can no longer position itself as aloof and authoritative but must be inclusive of a 'knowing' and more equal, style-savvy reader. Newspapers may still need to be 'informative' but new ways have to be found to do this, an aim in which designers have to play a big part.

4 Design and the Digital Media Environment

In this chapter, we draw on many of the fundamentals of design we have covered in the preceding chapters, but direct our focus at digital and mobile platforms. Web designers harness the same principles to load designs with specific ideas and attitudes as their colleagues working in print. But there are some considerations that apply to online design in particular. Designs must work cross-platform for brand consistency. They may have to take into account technical aspects such as browser compatibility and file size in relation to available bandwidth as this will impact on the speed with which, for example, a webpage will load. Often designs simply have to signify 'high-tech', especially in mobile viewing technology. As one interviewee working for the Yahoo! news website told us, consumers expect their newly purchased device to have more swishy graphics and a more interactive look than their old model.

The linking up of print and online parts of the design and production process is one of the biggest challenges. Digital sections of news organisations often operate in a way that is not easily integrated with older print sections. Interviewees told us that news outlets tend to bolt digital departments on to existing operations rather than looking at how existing resources can be and need to be adapted to create a more seamless and efficient whole. At the time of writing some of the leading news organisations in the UK were turning the industry into turmoil as they sought to finally move towards more integrated models (Macmillan, 2013; Sweney, 2013). The problem is that circulation, particularly of the local press, has already been in crisis for some time. One interviewee, regional digital editor of Trinity Mirror for the Midlands Marc Reeves, told us that much of what is currently being done in the industry was happening far too late as there has been complacency and a refusal to accept the commercial changes that are affecting the industry. The magazine industry also suffers from a lack of certainty in regard to the online and mobile models it might best use for different kinds of titles. Aside from aligning production processes, another big problem is how to monetise online content. Interviewee Loraine Davies of the Periodicals Training Council noted that many titles were being run increasingly by temporary staff with just sufficient technical skills, often being employed in preference to those with journalism training in order to save money. Such trends have huge influences on the quality of design.

As mentioned already, web and mobile design have much in common with print. In fact, the two feed off each other, with online design trends often feeding back into print. Perhaps most significantly, however, while digital technology freed up designers from the constrictions of earlier print technology, some designers feel that the web and mobile have brought in a new set of limitations.

We want to look first of all at how the emergence of digital platforms has changed the design process itself and at the technology that is involved. We then present four case studies: the online news site Yahoo!; the online version of *The Guardian* newspaper; the business-to-business magazine *Car Accessory Trader*; and the teenage magazine *Mizz*. In each case we speak with the designers and examine how these products have more recently been redesigned and the extent to which such designs are in the hands of technicians rather than designers.

Digital design and the power of technology

In the process of researching this area of design in journalism, one thing became immediately apparent: The onscreen world of digital media is a very amorphous one. It is not easy to establish merely from looking at newspaper and magazine websites, online news platforms and apps, how they have come about, who made them, who produces content for them and what goes on behind the actually visible page.

The hierarchy of jobs in a print environment became very established over the decades, and it was quite apparent who was involved in creating the look of any given print news title or magazine. But this is not so in the world of online news.

In some cases websites are created in-house by magazine and newspaper publishers. In other cases they are created by outside agencies that specialise in delivering web platforms to businesses. It may even be the case that an individual title has to work with a generic template provided by the publisher.

More experienced designers we spoke with across a number of media outlets felt that in some sense the digital environment had brought about a return to a former era where designers were reliant on what the printers said was possible for reasons of hardware and technology. In the early days of news and magazine publishing, layout was done by separate design agencies with the required technical skills and with very little input from editorial staff. This changed with the arrival of desktop publishing to the point where magazine and newspaper art directors now sometimes become editors and vice versa. But the shift to digital and the technical know-how required to implement digital designs has seen the power shift to those who have the technical knowledge to work with software, who don't necessarily have any journalism training, nor design expertise.

Ally Palmer, who was art director at the *Scotsman*, *Scotland on Sunday* and *The European*, before co-founding design agency PalmerWatson, says:

> In some ways it feels like we're back in the 80s before the impact of desktop publishing. In those days the editorial departments had limited control of what could or couldn't be done when it came to their content. The printers and pre-press areas (who put together the physical pages) had as much say as the editors. With the advent of desktop publishing and the Mac in particular in the late 80s and early 90s, control was wrestled away from pre-press and back to the editorial room. In many ways this was a golden period in newspaper design, with huge improvements in quality and a lot of innovation in design. Now it feels that control of digital design is very much in the hands of technical people and Content Management Systems making it harder, though not impossible, for the designer to have as great an influence.

While there are only two market-leading software packages to create print designs – Adobe InDesign and QuarkXpress – there are many different ways to produce webpages, many different kinds of software that can be used and many different programming languages that are constantly evolving. Creating apps too can involve up to ten or fifteen different pieces of software. This is another reason why tech-savvy people end up responsible for designing apps and websites.

Obviously those who operate the technology take their cues from editorial designers and editors, and try to recreate the brand of the print product as much as possible, mainly by using similar fonts and colour schemes. With improvements in technology and new developments in the way websites operate, this has become increasingly easy. There are no longer the same limitations on font use that created much difficulty in the early stages, for example. Ally Palmer says:

> Retaining a familiar look and feel of the print product online is difficult, with typographic control particularly challenging. There was a

time when you could safely use only a handful of fonts but now this is changing as more browser-safe fonts become available. It is also possible now to use the same fonts in print and online, which makes it possible to maintain a consistent look across both mediums.

There are some major differences between online and print design that impact greatly on the way news looks onscreen. Where newspapers have a complete redesign once every few years and stay virtually the same in between, websites exist in a much more fluid state. Their look can change even just by viewing them in different web browsers or on different devices. Individual page elements could move about, appear and disappear or change positioning depending on what device is used to view them. Pages can have indeterminate lengths, requiring cues for readers to explore outside of immediately visible boundaries. All of these characteristics bring new challenges to designers as they need to create good designs but also guide readers as to how they should be read. And different websites will have very different purposes. Some merely showcase the best content to push readers to buy the print edition. Some are fully fledged news platforms in their own right, presenting up-to-date content more frequently than their print counterpart and fulfilling more bespoke functions, especially in the case of apps. *What Car?* magazine, for example, launched a free car valuation app in August 2012 that allowed users to calculate the price of a used car by typing in a set of characteristics such as make, model and mileage.

Online design has to fulfil slightly different functions and objectives than print design by virtue of its practical differences. Online media play a different role in people's lives, are consumed and integrated into the world in different ways. Time spent on every online page on average is even shorter than that spent on any given printed page. The next more exciting thing is never more than a mouse-click away. So the reader needs to be encouraged to stay on the page for at least a certain amount of time.

Online-only news sites: The case of Yahoo!

The Yahoo! news site is based on immediacy. It is different from newspaper websites in that it is in the first place a news aggregator with various contracts with news agencies that supply it with stories that can be continually updated.

Yahoo! started as a search engine. Seeing what people would often search for gave the founders an insight into what kind of content was popular online. 'Hotmail' was a particularly popular search term. This led to the decision to provide a Yahoo!-based email service rather than sending people off to someone else's site. The news platform came about in a similar fashion: Yahoo! noticed a high amount of searches for football scores, celebrity names, stock prices, etc. A news agenda specific to Yahoo! users emerged, and again it was decided that this sort of content could be provided on the Yahoo! page without sending users elsewhere. Web and app designer Carrie Cousins told us that:

> While Yahoo! does borrow some characteristics from the websites of traditional newspapers, it still focuses on user-friendliness and quick information. Headlines are fun and engaging and written much more for the time-pressed over-extended reader than in the case of many traditional news sites. By combining both search and information gathering, Yahoo! has found a way to capitalise on news people want to read.

Original content has also been based on teasers and tit-bits to persuade readers to stay on the page. The priority, content creator Edward Bovingdon said, is to get people to spend time on the page.

The strength of Yahoo! is its ability to cope with enormous amount of web traffic to its site. Due to a vast number of people already using the platform to check emails and do searches, Yahoo! was set up to be able to handle large amounts of traffic. Newspaper platforms or even bbc.co.uk don't anticipate similar onslaughts from users. One of the first big breaking news events that tested relatively recently established news websites was 9/11. CNN and MSNBC's news servers experienced heavy traffic and collapsed only three minutes after the first plane hit the World Trade Center.

The Yahoo! website stayed live throughout. This was in part due to all advertising having been removed from the site very shortly after the news story broke. With the ad graphics removed, much less data needed to be transferred each time a user accessed the site, so it could continue operating. Advertisers were content to not have their products placed alongside such horror anyway.

Alick Mighall, Founder of miggle.co.uk, a web services provider that specialises in online content creation and management and has been involved with producing out-of-hours content for the Yahoo! website, explains what happened when the story of Michael Jackson's death broke:

> It was about 11pm in the UK when the first reliable source announced his death and at this point given the late night time, Yahoo! may be

one of the first UK news providers to cover the story. Every minute counts. A story like that has to be live within five minutes of it breaking. In those five minutes the appropriate picture for the target audience is chosen, a headline and teaser-text is written, the story is pulled from whichever agency, wire or other source broke the story to begin with, it is previewed and then published.

The level of certainty about the source of the story may be reflected in the design. If a celebrity dies and it's still just a rumour, there may be a simple 'Breaking News' in bolder letters next to the story. When it's all verified and certain, then it may turn into a different design with a more visible splash. At the time of writing there were maybe three or four special front-page designs for Yahoo! to use when big stories break, according to Mighall.

The main consideration is what the key business drivers are and what Yahoo! wants the site to do. So in a 2009 redesign the site was massively decluttered and stripped down, as there was a lot of duplication of different links in different places leading to the same thing. Looking into the way the site was used, it became obvious that while slideshows showing quirky pictures received many clicks, they didn't hold users' attention for very long. Yahoo! had to weigh this up against what services it wants its website to prioritise and also the preferences of advertisers. This is what the design reflects.

Two screenshots are shown, one of the Yahoo! website in 2006 (Figure 4.1) and then the site as it looked in July 2013 (Figure 4.3).

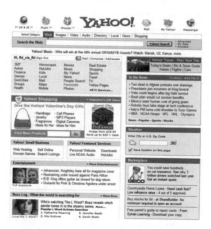

Figure 4.1   Yahoo! in 2006

We now look at some of the design changes in greater detail and in the context of the aims of the site. There has been a move away from an older sense of the internet where these search engine sites sought to represent themselves as portals and hubs of activity, a treasure chest of links. Now a more branded look is often demanded by advertisers. It is also characteristic of the matured web environment with savvier users with established site use patterns.

Fonts

We can see three major changes in the use of fonts from the old to the new design. First, as Carrie Cousins points out, we find a reduced number of fonts. She said: 'The use of a simple font palette makes the site seem more credible and news-like.' On the older Yahoo! page we find a greater variety of font sizes, which are not used in a specific way to create clear hierarchies or connections across the page. This adds to the busy look in contrast to the relative quietness of the new page. This busyness itself would have been appropriate for the older web environment, which needed to point to the quantity of possibilities. It needed to communicate that it contains a treasure chest of pathways and that it is the go-to site for a multitude of information. In the early days of the web there was a sense of bewilderment by users as to how to deal with and search the amount of content available. A handful of search engines like Web Crawler, Yahoo! and Google appeared. They presented dense lists of information, creating the impression that they were perfect hubs for starting off any web activity. But by more contemporary standards this appears very busy and inaccessible.

The fonts themselves have also changed. These were formerly more condensed and appear cramped by contemporary standards. On the new version they are much more spaced out. This older form of font would create problems for the current multi-platform design requirements where designers need to create a look that results in a consistent browsing experience across platforms and therefore maintains brand identity. The whole effect of shifting to the more expanded font can also make a site feel less dogmatic.

The newer fonts appear more in harmony with the ideology of technology that portable gadgets require. Mighall told us that while they need to be mindful of the memory required by software to carry out certain kinds of actions, it is important that compositions for tablets and iPhones, for example, connote something design-savvy and innovative. Space, modern-looking fonts and carefully designed icons as well as swiping actions must present a sense of being advanced. This includes connoting modernity in fonts as well as using them to imply the space and freedom that technology should bring. Looking at the 'Trending Now' section especially, and also at the news section of the new Yahoo! page, we can also see greater line spacing. The older Yahoo! page resembles an older page of text in density. It looks like a directory and simply would not work for newer portable technology.

Framing

Another key difference in the new design is the attention to structure, alignment and framing. The old site indeed looks cluttered with a large number of different lists, boxes and panels. In the newer design the elements create clear hierarchies that direct the readers' interest to particular points. A tile-look has been introduced, which is a popular look on tablet and mobile devices. The browser design uses the same look to generate consistency across different platforms.

In terms of structure the new Yahoo! site also obeys the rule of thirds much more than the older version, which would seem to indicate a more direct involvement of a designer. The rule of thirds has been commonly discussed in the analysis of photography, where we imagine a grid of nine rectangles, three by three, over an image. Research has shown that most attention is placed by viewers on the points where the gridlines intersect. We can see this in Figure 4.2, in an example from Cousins (2012b). In web designs we should try to place important information at these points, as can be seen for the two bands of text. The Google logo sits in the top left box, which has been shown to attract most attention of all the nine boxes. We see in the Yahoo! case the logo has shifted from a more central position to the top left. These rebrands clearly have the markings of a more sophisticated sense of design and communication.

In the new Yahoo! design the two carousels follow the intersections on the grid. The positioning of the top carousel means that the top left intersection will fall over the lead image. In the older version we find no such precise attention to positioning.

Alignment is also very different between the old and new versions. On the newer design we can look at the way that different headings and bodies of text line up with those below them. The text for 'Who's the man who just bought Fulham?' aligns with the bullets for the news items at the bottom. The 'Yahoo! sites' all align, as does the heading. The text for the lower carousel uses centred text to create balance and to avoid having to align. Looking at the different contents boxes and

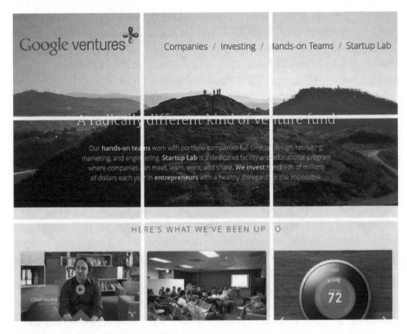

Figure 4.2   Webpage with salience gridlines
Source: Cited from Cousins, 2012b

headings of the older site, such clear alignments aren't immediately apparent. Sentences begin at many different places. For example, the Yahoo! 'Featured Services' does not align with the 'Yahoo! Shopping' headline nor with 'Entertainment'. The use of right-aligned text as in 'More Buzz' also adds to this jumbled look.

Colour

Colour is put to use in very different ways in the two sites. The old version uses a wider colour palette and there is no systematic attention to where colours are used. The new version uses three main colours systematically. The black/grey is used for much of the text but creates rhyming between the two carousels, which use this for reverse symmetry – the foreground in one case and background above. Cousins (2012b) pointed to the importance of this technique in contemporary design. This colour is also used for the fonts above the top carousel and above the search bar. This ordered and more measured use of colour brings salience to the blue and the brighter search bar.

Figure 4.3 Yahoo! in 2013

Newspaper sites: The design of *The Guardian* website

The Guardian was one of the first newspapers to take a more innovative approach to digital content and online news. Industry commentators such as former head of factual television at the BBC Jacquie Hughes have been very positive about its ability to contribute something slightly different to television news with its off-the-cuff video interviews and more spontaneous mobile phone footage complementing news stories that could not be carried by television bulletins in this fashion. We were able to ask designer Mark Porter and video journalist Shehani Fernando about the development of and changes to the site.

The Guardian was one of the first British newspapers to have a website in 1995. It was also one of the first newspapers to take its website design seriously, as Porter told us, hiring well-known graphic designer Neville Brody in 1998. Brody was asked to create a strong visual identity for the digital platform even though at this time technology still imposed serious limitations for content, with most people still using dial-up modems. Porter said that *The Guardian* was also thinking ahead of its time when the site was first discussed as even then there was a sense of how it could be used to maintain reader loyalty. Branding was already well established in the corporate world, but at this time newspapers hadn't really considered their look as a brand. In Figure 4.4 we see the site in 1999. There is a clear relationship with the newspaper, employing styles used for the newspapers itself and also the supplements. In the late 1990s other newspapers were often using much busier and content-heavy designs. This use of space and alignment was unique. The mustard and blue colour scheme is very much of its time, but feels dated now. So do the black and white images. The navigation at the top is still very simple, with only six different sections to choose from compared to the current top navigation that is divided into 13 sections, with the News section further broken down into 14 sections.

One of our interviewees, designer Ally Palmer, made the following observation about newspapers' attempts to maintain a brand across multiple platforms:

This can vary greatly between newspaper publishers. Some want to have an almost seamless look and feel between print and digital while others seek to keep them far apart. For some publishers it is enough to have the same name and to incorporate the newspaper logo on the top of the home page and for others they see it as one brand that should be unified across all formats, both print and digital. There was a time, due mainly to typographic restraints, that this was very difficult but that is rapidly changing.

Figure 4.4   The Guardian website in 1999

Figure 4.5 *The Guardian* website before and after the redesign of 2005

Mark Porter was in charge at the time of the major redesign of *The Guardian* newspaper in 2005. And it was at this time that it was decided that the website too needed an overhaul, with particular focus on its appearance as well as the underlying technology driving it (Figure 4.5).

The decision to implement a redesign was made by the then director of digital content, Emily Bell, and the paper's editor, Alan Rusbridger. With a website redesign there are often, as was the case here, two processes happening in parallel: the hardcore technical backdrop to the site gets a makeover as well as the front-end appearance. On the technical side this redesign marked the move away from using tables to structure the site and towards embracing Cascading Style Sheets (CSS). CSS is a way of writing the files used to encode websites (HTML files, for example) in such a way that the elements of the file regarding the look and presentation of the website (i.e. fonts, colours, layout) are kept separate from the content elements, which means several pages within a website can share the same presentation with minimum effort: They simply use the same bit of code for the form of the page – much like style sheets are used in print design – but then populate them with different words and pictures. Sites using CSS were more flexible, accessible and allowed for more control in specifying presentation characteristics as compared to the more rigid requirements of the table-driven design.

As *The Guardian* is Trust-owned, Porter said, there is a huge emphasis on openness and accessibility, something that was very pertinent in redesigning the website. The site has to be compatible across a wide range of browsers and devices, and readable and accessible by as many people with as many different viewing requirements as possible.

To reflect the amount of work required on the technical side versus the design side, it is telling that this website redesign project involved 50 programmers and only three or four designers. Mark Porter describes how designing for the web and other digital platforms has changed his working process, saying that he has to collaborate much more with people with relevant programming skills, whereas as an art director on a magazine or newspaper he could produce pages in InDesign without any other technical help.

The thinking behind the look of the page goes back to the same basic idea the print product is built on. Mark Porter said:

> There are fundamental principles of editorial design which I apply equally to everything. It has to be readable and navigable. The job of any editorial design is to allow the audience to engage with the content in as easy and enjoyable a way as possible.

Porter added that large and good-quality photographs had always been important in the printed edition of *The Guardian* and were to feature in a similar way on the new-look website. A similar design language as in the print version, regarding colour, image choice, typography and the use of space, was to be used online. An architecture built around tags and teasers became a significant part of the new website, and videos and podcasts were to become more frequently used features. We can see the difference between the websites after the redesign. We find fewer images and blocks of colour, and a massive increase in space. As was also the case for the Yahoo! website described above, there has been a much more careful use of salience and alignment. On the older site blocks of colour used to frame images compete for attention, and poorer alignment makes it seem hard work for the eye. The four basic blocks of content are all slightly different widths on the screen. These problems have been resolved in the redesign. The new design uses salient colours in the fashion of more modern newspapers: not to draw attention to a specific item but in their textual function of bringing shape and liveliness to the page. But this is done often quite discreetly, as we saw with the *Evening Standard* redesign where one lively colour might be used for a colour bar and then used in subtle highlights for other items to create rhyme. And, as with the *Standard*, we find the introduction of brighter colours, moving towards those formerly used more in magazine design. There is also a more limited range of image sizes and positioning, as with the Yahoo! site.

One important part of the shift to online, again showing the newspaper's sense of innovation at the time, was to include original video material and reports. While these could not compete in terms of quality with TV news outlets, they still warranted the creation of a dedicated department within *The Guardian* that was responsible for the production of video content. Shehani Fernando was part of the first wave of journalists working on this part of the site. She had a background of working for BBC London News as a camera woman and was part of a team of four staff producing video content.

Integrating online content production into the existing working structure of a daily national newspaper was an interesting process in itself. Shehani says:

When I first joined, *The Guardian* was in the old building in Farringdon. The whole of the digital operation had been put into the top floor and physically away from the print operation. At first this created lots of difficulties. Later a move to new premises did lead to more integration in terms of reporters and writers. The video and audio production team, however, were still separate and sitting together in one multimedia area. And importantly they were general reporters covering stories across different subject areas, which differed from how other sections of the newspaper operated.

In the early days, Shehani says, it felt very much like the video team was working in isolation. There were no clear lines of communication between print journalists, editors and the video team, and no clear strategy as to who could make use of the video department or how. Over time links did begin to emerge, and now she feels print and video have become firmly interlinked. The news video editor will go to the news conferences and there's much more forward planning in line with what print journalists are planning on covering. This meant it was possible to think about how the video can add additional elements to a story such as showing interviews. Video and print teams are much more on each other's radar and the collaboration is much stronger.

There were other changes for print journalists as they found themselves having to take on completely new roles for which they had no training, such as being news presenters. Shehani said that:

If you were hired as a print journalist to suddenly be told you need to engage in multi-media, video and podcasting – the amount of stuff a *Guardian* journalist has to do now is much more than they had to do eight or ten years ago. But some people really flourished and were fantastic at it.

And, as we found across many of our interviews it was those able to turn their hand to a range of skills that had the best chance to find employment. At the time of writing, large companies such as Trinity Mirror, while laying off print journalists, were taking on new staff with digital skills. This included a raft of positions in senior management. One of our interviewees, Marc Reeves, had just been appointed regional digital editor for the Midlands in the UK at the time of writing. And these new roles often demonstrated the company's intentions to turn from a traditional news organisation into a multimedia business.

While publications often still seem to struggle with how to generate revenue from online platforms, *The Guardian*'s video department was making money, because it was running so-called pre-roll ads that – much like TV ads – play before the bit of news-footage a reader may have chosen to view. This allows for expansion and further efforts to establish more of this sort of content on the site. For example, Shehani talked about the importance of stand-alone interactive pieces that usually incorporate a long-format feature article and many other multimedia elements such as video, audio and graphics.

But the success of the videos and of the website as a multimedia platform hinged on an editor's sense of how to use this content. The success of videos, Shehani says, was very much dependent on just how much billing they got in the paper and where they were linked into the website. Videos that were placed high up on the home page would obviously receive a lot of plays. And leading figures in the news industry, such as Jacquie Hughes of the BBC, said that while *The Guardian* website often contained excellent material, it was not always obvious to readers that it was there.

In terms of visual style, the video team received no briefs or instructions. *The Guardian* didn't set out to create a 'Guardian' style for its videos and, indeed, video footage on the website takes diverse forms. In many ways a lot of coverage followed old-school TV news conventions. Shehani says: 'That was a debate to be had whether Web TV should be like TV or should be different. The joy of it was that it was all very experimental.' Not being TV does open opportunities for unusual ways of covering events, which ends up shaping the look of the footage produced. For example, for live unfolding news events, such as a demonstration, a member of the video team might go along with a mobile phone and use that to record some footage and instantly upload it to *The Guardian* YouTube channel from where it can then be embedded onto the website.

Figure 4.6   Screenshot from *The Guardian*, 2008

A TV camera obviously doesn't provide the same opportunity for and feel of immediacy. And it is the kind of content that may not be usable for a mainstream news programme.

A screenshot from November 2008 shows that the new design has been refined further (Figure 4.6). As mentioned before, online designs tend to be more continually in flux as compared to print newspapers, which undergo design overhauls much less frequently. The new masthead design of the redesigned print paper at the time has been echoed on the website, with guardian.co.uk being spelt out in the two tones of blue that are used for 'the' and 'guardian' on the front page. The all-lower-case look of the name is a very recognisable feature of the brand, and it looks less formal than the former 'Guardian Unlimited' with upper-case initials. Another major change in design is the further improvement of the navigation menu across the top. The sections are now colour-coded and all in one line at the top, whereas specific news topics are in a second line underneath, with a very slight grey tint setting them off from the white background.

The spacing is more carefully thought out, with text and links belonging to the same story being grouped closely together with a bigger gap and also a thin grey divider line separating off the next story. The spacing in the menu panel on the right also appears to be more effective and pleasing.

The multimodality of line spacing and text alignment

As well as font shapes there is also meaning potential in line spacing and alignment of text (Lupton, 2010). We can draw upon this to think a little more about the interpersonal function of typography, about the mood or attitude it can convey and the ideas it communicates. We have seen these meaning potentials harnessed particularly on the newer newspaper and web designs to create a sense of 'room to think' and openness.

Spacing

Line spacing, also known in print terminology as leading, is the distance between the baseline of one line of type to the baseline of the next. This can have the same metaphorical association as expansion in the case of letters being spaced out horizontally from each other in individual words. When the gap is small there can be the impression of claustrophobia, of crowding, or also of economy. Wider spaces can mean more expansive, confident, or also greedy and even arrogant. But this sense of space can draw heavily on associations of modernism and open spaces. We find this in corporate entrance halls, designer cafés or clothes shops. Letters on a museum of modern art will most likely be spaced out as opposed to pushed together, which would suggest something more 'buttoned-up', condensed and with a greater unity of ideas and attitudes. In designer shops in large cities, we find huge expanses of empty, clean, polished floors with just a few expensive items placed, themselves apart from other items, giving a very different impression from a cheap shop where shoes are cramped together on shelves. In designer cafés there is much space, where tables and sofas are positioned far apart to create an impression of minimalism. Here there are associations of modernism, of the economy of design features, also the luxury of space. Lupton (2010: 83) notes that once line spacing becomes more extreme the lines begin to appear as separate. Space can also metaphorically represent the peace and relaxation, the ease that is also a feature of minimalism and large airy rooms.

What is clear here is that space communicates both ideas about luxury and modernity but also communicates at an interpersonal

(*continued*)

level in terms of attitude and moods. So in cases of space between lines a communicator can express confidence or a relaxed, unhurried mood. On the Google Ventures webpage we see space between the title and the text, which also uses spacing. Metaphorically it rhymes with the open space in the photograph. Like the photograph, it also suggests room to think and operate.

Text alignment

Alignment of typeface is something we are familiar with on our word processors through the term 'justified'. Yet we may not be familiar with thinking about it in terms of meaning potential. Consider the following examples:

The text of this book uses the so-called justified alignment for the bulk of its text meaning the left and right edges are even. It appears bordered and regimented. Broadsheet newspapers use this type of alignment to bring an attitude of efficiency, authority and formality.

In this paragraph the left edge is even whereas the right is not.
It creates a slightly more informal look, and is favoured by more
modern newspaper designs and webpages. It can look slightly
more organic. The words can take up the space that they wish as
opposed to being forced into a particular shape, and gaps between
the words are even. The mood and attitude that emerges is slightly
more natural and relaxed.

In this paragraph the left is ragged but the right is even. Since
in the West written language is read from the right this makes
it slightly more difficult to follow. Each line takes up a different
position. The text looks less formal. It does not want to be easy to
read. It wants you to work at it. We might say that by association
a confident attitude is conveyed. It says what it has to say with
conviction. There is a sense of a commentary that is important. It
is also used to provide textual coherence in right-hand marginal
notes. Using right-aligned text can suggest something slightly
creative and edgy. On webpages designers may place a section of
text like this to the bottom right of a page to add a note of creativity. Text that is aligned on the right is also very good at attracting
attention as it is much less commonly used than justified or left-aligned text.

(*continued*)

This piece of text is symmetrical. Both edges are ragged yet
provide a balance. We are familiar
with finding centred text such as this on invitations,
commemorative plaques or greetings cards. There can be a sense
of history, formality and tradition here.
This can be given even greater gravity by increasing
line spacing. The Google Venture webpage above uses this type
of text formatting to communicate
a sense of invitation and also something a little
more momentous. Yet it does not feel too formal as it is
combined with other
elements that point to space and openness.
This
piece of text
is staggered with both edges
ragged but without symmetry.
It has the effect of stuttering, of broken rhythm,
where each burst may indicate a separate thought.
Or of playfulness or fun.
This formatting
would be more difficult to use on webpages if they need to
contain more information, such as a news site.
Designer Ron Reason told us that he liked to play around with text
alignment in this way. But he noted that the designer needs to be
very careful about the ideas and attitudes that this communicates
and the extent to which it suits the brand.

Designing a site for magazines: The case of *Car Accessory Trader*

In this section we look at the process and sequences of decisions that lie behind the development of a website for a print publication. While some publishers have their own web design staff, others do not and may bring in specialists. This was the case for the magazine *Car Accessory Trader* published by Haymarket. We want to look at the development of the online version from the viewpoint of the in-house designer, in fact one of the authors, who was able to observe the process of the magazine going online as part of her regular involvement with the title. We also interviewed Roger Barr, head of Lion Digital, the web publishers who created the magazine's online presence, who told us about the kinds of work they carried out for publishers. This could involve supporting magazines in putting their own designs online, or even produce the web designs themselves from scratch. The agency would also provide advice on how to promote the website along with print versions, drive more traffic in its direction and foster the online brand.

Lion Digital is fundamentally a Wordpress agency. It uses a software package provided by Wordpress to assemble sites. A huge amount of different software components called PlugIns come with this software. These allow access to functions such as linking to social media, using spam checkers and embedding of other media, such as videos from YouTube. It is not therefore necessary to write the entire code for each website from scratch, but a case of choosing from a range of building blocks. At the lower-budget end of the production of web versions of titles we found that online design companies provide complete online magazine templates as well as templates for print versions under a number of themes, such as IT, Extreme, Lifestyle. All these come complete with fonts, colours, layouts and graphics into which a publisher can drop its own content.

One of the authors is the designer on *Car Accessory Trader* (*CAT*) magazine, a business-to-business title for the car parts manufacturing and distribution industry, and responsible for all editorial page layout in a freelance capacity. She was also involved in a redesign in 2011 implemented in collaboration with Gene Cornelius, art director of *Management Today*.

CAT has a circulation of around 17,000 and is targeted at executives in the car parts industry. This includes garage owners as well as the CEOs of large brands such as Delphi, Denso and Bosch. The redesign took this into account, and the aim was to create a look that would be serious and corporate and yet use some more informal elements, too.

Around the same time as the redesign, *CAT* magazine was approached by Lion Digital who proposed to set up and host a website version of the magazine. *CAT*'s designer attended one meeting with representatives of Lion Digital, the publishing director and the editor of *CAT* that set the direction for the visual appearance of the site.

At the time of the meeting many other Haymarket magazines had already developed online versions. At *CAT* it had been felt that the readership didn't consist of the kind of people who spent much time in front of computers or surfing the net as they weren't necessarily office-based. But as mobile surfing devices had become increasingly more widespread, websites became more interesting for *CAT*'s advertisers.

At the meeting Lion Digital showed print-outs of what the webpage might look like. In its draft design it had used some of the elements of the *CAT* branding to link with the print version, such as the logo and the signature colours. It was agreed that Lion Digital would put together the site and host it for the magazine. The page's CMS allows editorial staff to change words and pictures and update the blog. But the location of page elements stays the same. Beyond that the designer, editor or publisher of the magazine had no further involvement with the design of the website. It was felt that Lion Digital understood the brand well enough and that the draft it had created maintained the brand's look sufficiently.

Occasionally the publishing director or editor will request changes to be made to the layout of the website in response to new elements or sections being required. The website content is regularly updated throughout the magazine's monthly production cycle. But there is no real design input or involvement from the magazine designer who, in this case, had no experience of web design and programming and so did not know what was, and was not achievable in terms of the website's look. As in the age of the dominance of expert printing staff over typesetting and the look of newspaper pages, it is difficult for editorial staff to challenge what is presented by web programming experts as best practice. And what quickly becomes the overriding concern for editors and reporting staff is the usability of the CMS and whether what they input will be configured consistently.

Figure 4.7 shows the website, which can be compared to the print version seen in Figure 4.8. There are a number of important differences,

Figure 4.7   CAT magazine website

Figure 4.8   CAT magazine print version

which point to the value of websites and also key ways in which the look of the brand has been maintained.

First, the website brings together content in one place that appears on separate pages in the print version. The magazine produces a mini telephone book-style directory of companies within the industry, listing their contact information. This is simply incorporated into the site as a separate section. The same is done for the Catalogue Guide supplement, which used to be produced on a bi-yearly basis. Software allows this to be easily and quickly updated, which is one standard user expectation of websites. The advice was to foreground this as part of the services offered by the site. The print version still resembles much more of a typical subject- and features-driven cover. To give the site energy a carousel has been used on its home page with a rotating image and mobile text, which rises for each story.

The visual branding has been done by maintaining logos and colours although, as Roger Barr mentioned, this was often the toughest part as he would have to work with colours and fonts that would be recognised by browsers. Often this meant using approximations. Where the print magazine was undergoing a redesign at the same time colours in the print version could be chosen to be compatible for use on the web version. The red on the *CAT* webpage is slightly different from the printed red. Where necessary, as in the case of logos, fonts can be reproduced by rendering these as a picture. Barr pointed out newer software and newer browsers are affording designs the ability to carry with them instructions about kinds of fonts and colours. The browser will then pick from a range of fonts available on any given computer that is trying to access a site. It builds in more versatility as fonts that have to be carried as an image can then lead to problems, with the appearance of the site being adjusted for different screen sizes.

The website has also been given more generic sans serif fonts for the list of products, where in the magazine a light version of Griffith Gothic is used, which is slightly more playful in its use of wider and narrower lines. The generic sans serif, however, helps with the clean look of the website.

Other signature elements of the print design have been incorporated into the look of the website, such as the little red squares that are used as bullet points throughout the magazine and as seen in Figure 4.9 the arrows that are used to create energy. These are transferred to the website for the 'read more' buttons.

The webpage is also influenced by tablet requirements, with a slight tiled look and an intentional use of space bordering all of the elements.

The tile look also goes along with a much more extensive use of teaser boxes. According to page editors, a new kind of writing has emerged for these teasers, which need to withhold as much information as they actually reveal to you. These accompany the white-on-red arrow pointing to the 'read more' link. These features become even more important on tablet versions where a tile look will also need to encourage the user to swipe in different directions.

Advertisements on the site, such as the so-called 'site skin' visible in Figure 4.7 featuring semicircles and pictures of computer and tablet screens, were managed with the OpenX system. This can be used to sell

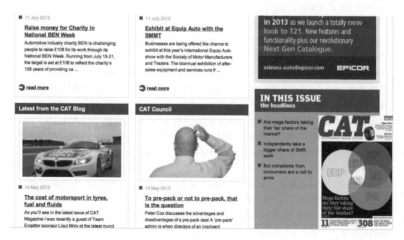

Figure 4.9   CAT web branding details

and manage advertising space as well as take payments. The software can allow adverts to change or to be made larger or smaller depending on the profile of the viewer. But this also means that the designer cannot visualise how the page will finally be seen by the viewer.

Mizz magazine

Further down the rankings of control over web design we find magazines like *Mizz* aimed at teenage girls. This is a piece of research carried out by Eleanor Perkins, a journalism student at Brunel University, London. *Mizz* magazine has to rely on a fixed template provided by the publisher, which staff feel is not particularly well aligned with the look of the magazine itself. Of course publishers have to balance investments with the strength of titles.

Mizz is run by a full-time staff of five, half the number it used to be, who are also involved in the production of a range of other titles. What is notable in this case are declining sales of the print copy and the increased need to use social media along with the web to engage with a newer generation of readers who have no established culture of buying magazines.

The magazine's editor, Karen O'Brien, said that the future of all teen magazines looked bleak. The past three years had witnessed a steady decline in the entire market and many were running at a loss as teens turn to more immediate information available online. The titles tend to have a high cover price due to the need to carry free gifts. Distribution is also expensive, with distributors Marketforce taking a 50% cut of *Mizz*'s sales.

The title was originally published by IPC Media and then purchased by Panini Comics in 2006. Panini Comics at the time was the fourth largest publisher of juvenile titles in Europe. The magazine was fortnightly, but went to monthly in 2012. It was at this point that the website was launched by the new owners.

Of the handful of staff design is in the hands of Carol Bateup, who also works on other titles such as *Just Pop* and *Disney Presents*. She has worked at Panini UK for five years, but on *Mizz* for two years. Bateup uses design templates to maintain *Mizz*'s style and look in every issue. Approximately 40% of the magazine is templated, including the contents page, the quizzes and the horoscopes page. What most frustrates Bateup, however, is that *Mizz* has little control over its website. The site is very structured and does not have any video content. As we saw above

Figure 4.10   Mizz magazine website, with strict template

in the case of the sites provided by Lion Digital, customers would have to choose from a range of PlugIns depending on what they wanted to achieve. This would include things like links to social media, management of advertisements and video embedding. The site provided had none of these (Figure 4.10).

Feature writer Claire Norman stressed: 'We've had to set up our own YouTube channel so we could get video content. That way we can show interviews.' Claire had taken on much of the online activity, editing videos of interviews after carrying them out and then uploading them to YouTube. She would also use Twitter to announce competitions and winners, to promote interviews and interact with other Twitter feeds such as *Just Pop* to direct traffic to *Mizz* for related content. Norman is National Council for the Training of Journalists (NCTJ)-trained but has had to learn editing and the web on the job. And this points to observations on magazine employment by industry leaders. Loraine Davies, director of the Periodicals Training Council in the UK, told us there was very little funding for training available from the publishers considering the comparatively extensive need for reskilling that the migration to digital platforms could be argued to require.

A further problem for the *Mizz* website is that it simply does not have the staff to provide regular updates. Much of the content is out of date and not acceptable given audience expectations. Norman said: 'I think websites need to be updated daily if not three times a day.' Nor is the site interactive, as is the case with more successful titles. Editor Karen O'Brien said that such sites would have space for reader engagement, opinions and analytics. They would have celeb news constantly being updated and featured. They would be able to run interviews when PRs ring to ask if something can be put online. The *Mizz* site is simply too structured. O'Brien said, 'We know kids are going on apps and tablets but we don't have anything like that.' But she acknowledged that given the falling sales and the fact that since some of their readers might be as young as ten, it is tougher to take the online market for granted.

Apps

The most recent development in visual journalism, and one that only just started taking place as this book was being written, was the arrival of newspaper and magazine apps for tablet computers. While early experiments with handheld computer devices, such as ultra mobile PCs, personal digital assistants and Palm Pilots, go back as far as the 1990s, it was not until 2002 that Microsoft attempted to launch a tablet device, but these were too heavy to hold with one hand for any length of time. In 2008 the first Android tablets appeared, but it was the Apple counterpart – the iPad – released on April 3, 2010, roughly around the time research for this book began, that proved to be game-changing and have since defined and shaped the tablet market. And it wasn't long before people we interviewed about their magazine or newspaper design work started mentioning that their publication's latest project was to make an app. In some cases large sums of money were invested. And the wonderfully crisp screen of the iPad lends itself well to showing off magazine content. But – as in the early days of web publishing – it was proving difficult to generate revenue from tablet publishing. Keith Martin writes in *MacUser* magazine, June 2013:

> According to a report on paidcontent.org, 289 US magazines sold a combined total of 7.9 million digital copies in the second half of 2012. Impressive, but that was just 2.4% of their total (print and digital) circulation. Looking at the UK, *Men's Health* is the biggest selling paid-for men's title here, according to the PPA, and in that July–December period last year [2012] it averaged 12,676 digital copies a month. That's good, but hardly a challenge to the monthly print circulation of 202,704.

At the time of this book going to press it was still difficult to make any kind of guess as to where apps were headed. Were they just a fad quickly embraced by progressive publishers ever eager to stay ahead of the latest digital trend? Or would they – as some have indeed suggested – replace the print editions of newspapers and magazines eventually?

Ed Chamberlin, who works for international travel publishers INK Global, and has been designing apps for some of the company's in-flight and on-train magazines, says: 'I don't think people associate their iPads with reading magazines really.'

In 2011 Apple launched Newsstand – an in-built application for iPhones, iPads and iPod Touch – which ships with the device and cannot be deleted. It allows users to download and display app versions of newspapers and magazines. Ed has observed that of all the people whose iPads or iPhones he gets to see, he has never seen anyone who has anything waiting to be read in their Newsstand. Granted this is not exactly empirical evidence, but it would seem to suggest that great enthusiasm about apps being the holy grail of generating new revenue for ailing print publishers may be misplaced.

Mark Porter has a different take on it. He thought there was a chance that apps may supersede print publications. He says about the *Guardian* app:

> The philosophy of it was to be much more like print. The brief was to create an experience that has everything that is good about print, but that feels as if it belongs on the iPad. And we thought very hard about this. And for me it came down to two things: One was that when you read a printed newspaper it has a hierarchy. The editor makes a decision about what's the most important story, what's the next important story and what's the least important story. And when people buy a newspaper, they don't just buy the stories that are in the newspaper, they buy the editor's judgement about the stories. The other thing people love about newspapers is that they can get an overview. They can sit with a 32 page newspaper, turn all the pages and get a grasp of everything that's in there... and then you can get a feel what you want to go back to and read. So we wanted to capture that.

Ally Palmer echoes that sentiment with the following comment:

> Like any editorial content, digital design needs structure and hierarchy. Although it is much harder to control the path a user may take (in print it is an obvious process of turning pages) you still need to create a design that ensures that wherever a user is, they can find

relevant content that may interest them as well as an easy navigation that allows them to find other sections and other types of content.

The *Guardian* app is published daily, with only the content of the print edition rather than being constantly updated like the website, because it was felt that there was a certain audience that wanted that much more print-like experience. And that's where Mark Porter sees the future of apps. With the readership of print newspapers in decline almost all over the world, he still feels that high-quality journalism is in demand and needs to be provided in various forms, with apps being one.

American designer Carrie Cousins says:

Print and online are different mediums and there is value in treating them differently, but I should recognise a newspaper immediately whether I am looking at it in print or online. One newspaper that is thinking ahead of the curve when it comes to design is *The Boston Globe* which is one of the first (if not *the* first) newspaper site to use responsive design. What the *Globe* is doing is creating a universal news experience – in print, on desktops, on tablets and on mobile phones. The *Globe* also uses its typefaces (or similar versions) online and in print, creating simple and effective branding across platforms. The overall design is nothing that knocks your socks off, but is simple, clean, readable and usable.

But the problem for these news outlets, as head of Trinity Media Simon Fox told us, is not so much what can be done with the technologies and platforms but how to pay for them. In the present environment websites and apps may well get huge traffic, but this is not so useful if it is still the print version that is relied upon for revenue.

The *FT*, too, has an app version. Again it creates a more print-like rather than browser-like experience. Its pages are of fixed height, so the layouts are only as big as the screen. Much like on newspaper front pages, ellipses are added in, indicating that there is more text on this story elsewhere. A tap will then take the reader to the rest of the story. As simple as that may seem, it is actually a bespoke bit of software called the FTEllipsis library that makes this possible with multiple-line-pieces of text.

Cousins sums up what makes good online news design successful:

Newspapers don't need to reinvent the (design) wheel online. Use colours, fonts and a design philosophy that matches the tone of the printed paper online as well. Opt for type and voice that has a complementary style. Does your paper use big, bold images in print? The same should be done online. Is your paper's style soft and airy or tight? The web should also have a mirroring feel. You want readers to connect with the newspaper brand on every device.

Three distinct types of magazine apps seem to be emerging. The first one is nothing much more than a slideshow of all the pages of the print magazine displayed on a tablet rather than printed on paper. These are very easy to generate from the existing PDFs of the magazine or newspaper. There is little interactivity and no multimedia content. The problem is that engaging with something presented in an interactive screen medium makes users expect to be able to engage with it in a particular way. Merely swiping through magazine pages in chronological order doesn't constitute a tablet experience. As we saw in our analysis of Yahoo!, designs often need to fit with high-tech connotations of applications.

More ambitious magazines are producing bespoke iPad editions of their publications. These are new iterations of the layout custom-shaped to fit the iPad screen and to work well with the available space. The page layout changes depending on which way round the device is turned. Some images are actually videos that play upon tapping, and the opening layout of a feature may in fact be a slideshow, so the reader can swipe through and pick from a selection of opening images. *Time* magazine is a very good example of one such app, producing it very early on in the history of the iPad – it certainly created a true iPad experience that delivers something above and beyond what a print product can.

But there is also a third kind of app, which takes a given magazine or its readership or subject matter as a starting point, but doesn't really attempt to be a magazine at all. The award-winning *BBC GoodFood* app, for example, comes in the form of recipe cards. One 'side' of the card will show a picture and the name of the dish. Swiping it makes the card appear to flip over and reveal the ingredients and step-by-step instructions on the back. There is an overall picture-led menu of all the dishes to choose from. At the time of making, the flipping-over animation of the recipe cards was something that hadn't been done before and code had to be written specially to be able to do it.

Another similar magazine-related app was produced by *What Car?*, as previously mentioned. It allows the user to input a second-hand car's registration, make and model, and based on that will work out what the car's price should be – a truly useful tool for a reader of *What Car?*

This last category of apps is much more in line with what apps are good at: performing little tasks such as finding directions, checking cinema listings or managing your fitness regime. So perhaps apps may be more useful as add-ons to the existing publication rather than as something that tries to emulate the publication itself.

Aggregators

At the time of writing aggregator apps had also only just started appearing as a way of viewing news media on tablet devices and smart phones (Figure 4.11). They are a reflection of the fluidity of the online publishing world as they go beyond individual brands and present stories from various online newspaper and magazine sources, sort them into categories and give the reader a dashboard through which to navigate to their favourite content. Ally Palmer says about them:

> Now we are beginning to see more distinctive digital designs that in many ways reflect the look and feel of different types of content providers. So sites like Flipboard and Pulse which aggregate news and are hugely popular with a younger content consumer, are starting to influence more established content providers like the BBC and *The Guardian*.

Pulse was created by two graduate students from Stanford University. Their aim was to revolutionise the news reading experience. Their app

Figure 4.11   Flipboard mobile phone aggregator

won the Apple Design Award and had 30 million users in July 2013, a figure that was allegedly growing by a million a month at the time.

For designers this might, of course, mean that what they produce will always be formatted to the styles of the aggregator, as in the case of Yahoo!. And it may also mean that readers will no longer expect to access content through a front entrance as they did formerly, as instead it will be found on aggregators. The challenge for individual outlets is to create a strong brand through all their material for recognition by site visitors. At the time of writing it was exactly these kinds of problems that all the big publishers were considering, leading to changing identities of some of the larger outlets.

Conclusion

In the previous chapter we saw how digital technology served to free up designers from what was felt to be limitations imposed by printers. In this chapter, we have seen a shift in the role of design online as the web has changed from an adventure to a mass medium where users have favoured sites and expect high standards. The emergence and growth of multimedia publishing has brought about the idea of branded design, with titles needing to have consistency across platforms. A newer specialist digital designer has evolved from that who has to think in new ways about the visual presentation of news content. But this has come alongside a switch back to a situation where designers must refer to technical experts to have their designs implemented. It is web programming specialists who will know what can be done visually, given that browsers may not recognise some design features, have restraints on the file size that certain visual elements require, and that a large variety of devices may be used to view the content.

Costs and uncertainty as to what business models are likely to work in the changing news and magazine market have led also to an increased use in ready-made templates. While being a useful cost-saving measure these force in-house designers to work within very restricted pre-existing frameworks. But the appearance of any given medium's output may be more and more out of the hands of content creators at magazines, newspapers and TV stations. Rather than being accessed through their 'front doors' the viewing public may soon find their content through an increasingly diverse range of entry points such as social media and news aggregator apps.

5 Staging the News for Television

Television news is unique compared to other forms of visual journalism in that it shows the viewers what journalists look like and how they behave. It also gives them a sense of what news gathering entails and an opportunity to see journalists engaged in part of that process. Television news, it has been argued, is important also because television is itself so fused into people's everyday lives in a way that is different from other news genres (McKay and Ivey, 2004; Briggs, 2009). Television personalities become part of the domestic environment to a special, very intimate extent. It is partly this close relationship with the people who deliver television news that gives it so much force and impact on viewers (Hartley, 1996).

But the visual language that television news uses to communicate about world events and to generate meaning is less frequently investigated. In this chapter we begin by looking at the introductory sequences of news bulletins, how they have changed over time and how these connote different and shifting ideas of the meaning of news and journalism. We then look at how news set designs, which themselves have changed over time, communicate specific ideas and attitudes about news. Finally, we examine a typical news package as it reports on a political press release. In this chapter we carry out an analysis of television news from a multimodal perspective, drawing on interviews with the designers of introductory sequences, sets and news editors, as well as observations of the news production process.

The changing television news-scape

Television news remains the most trusted and accessed form of news around the world, for political coverage, disasters and war (Ursell, 2003; Cushion, 2012). At the end of the first decade of the 21st century 15 million people were still watching the evening news in the UK (Ofcom, 2010), over 24 million in the US (Pew, 2010), 45 million in India, despite the ownership of TV being only just over twice this number (Lakshmi, 2007), and over 200 million in China (Hayes, 2010). And it has been argued that it is television news that is most influential when it comes to political opinion (Wring and Ward, 2010). It is clear, however, that at this time there has been a drop in viewers, particularly younger viewers (Wayne et al., 2010) along with audience fragmentation (Project for Excellence in Journalism, 2011), for a range of reasons. Channels have multiplied, online and social media news has grown, and wider information consumption and leisure patterns are changing. But certainly television news remains widely viewed and highly influential, especially around key events, being increasingly fused with other media genres (Peters, 2010). This also needs to be placed in the broader context of the commercialisation of news, of increased competition between news bulletins and news channels, and also in the environment of increasing conglomeration, syndication and massive staff reductions. At the time of writing this is transforming both the BBC (Huffington Post, 2013) and ITV news (Kanter, 2012) in the UK.

News has also had to change as society itself has shifted in its sense of formality and its relationship to authority. As the boundaries between former media genres have blurred and citizens are increasingly understood as consumers, a lifestyle culture has emerged hand in hand with its doctrine of choice. We have already seen in Chapter 2 how these developments have influenced newspaper design.

All of these changes can, to some extent, be tracked through the analysis of the ways that news has presented itself visually over time (Ekström and Kroon Lundell, 2011). In an interview, BBC World News editor Julien Cousins told us that even over the last decade the BBC had been transforming its appearance and content as market research has shown that viewers found it overly formal and boring. BBC News editor Peter Day, when we interviewed him, said that changes in the news opening sequence and set redesign were part of creating a more 'contemporary look' and an international brand, and also developing a look that was more family-oriented. In 2008 the BBC changed its title sequence as part of a £550,000 rebranding of the overall news service carried out by branding agency Lambie Nairn. But what such practitioners tend to find harder to explain precisely is what it is that constitutes a 'contemporary' look and why exactly news should want to appear as more 'family-oriented'. What does this mean for the way that society shares and values knowledge and information, and who should provide this?

News opening sequences

There has been a massive change in the possibilities for television news introductions, from the use of basic animations to the versatile graphics and editing software that has emerged since about 2005, which makes it relatively easy to have text and images spinning around the screen. While some bigger news outlets will use their own designers, smaller organisations can use packages of ready-made opening sequences that can be cheaply purchased and personalised with software like AfterEffects and Adobe Premier. Nevertheless it remains important to look at what kinds of features and elements we find in these templates. However versatile or restricting a technology is, the choices made in visual elements still tell us what kinds of ideas, attitudes and values the designer feels should be loaded on to news.

Henry Cassirer, the first news picture editor on CBS in 1944, wrote extensively on his thoughts about visually representing the news and about how it should be introduced. Even at this early point in TV news history we find simple staging devices to help load meanings on to the news viewing experience. In the late 1940s NBC started with a view of a curtain, which then shifted to a board carrying the words 'The news with Clifton Utley'. This board then turns out to be a door, which opens and Utley introduces himself, looking like he is a movie news editor sitting on a bare wooden chair behind a desk. The camera enters and he reads the news in front of a world map. Utley wears a heavy tweed suit and, although remaining formal, appears far from the very serious official newsreaders that came later in the 1960s and 1970s as he casually sits comfortably with his arms folded and resting on the desk in front of him as he smiles slightly. He looks more like a schoolboy waiting for a lesson to start (Figure 5.1).

It is jarring to watch news sequences stemming from a time when TV news conventions we are now intimately familiar with hadn't yet been established. One edition of the NBC news programme (March 17, 1949) begins without any instructions as to what is contained in the bulletin and launches straight into an item about car prices. Notably there is no indication here as to the overall significance of the event (http://www. youtube.com/watch?v=1WkSM54iQRk).

We can get a sense of the changing ideas and attitudes being loaded on to news if we look at opening sequences across time, mainly in the UK context. In the 1950s and 1960s BBC news bulletins relied on images that symbolised the actual actions of news transmission. Very early news used an image of a radio transmission tower where the words 'BBC

Figure 5.1   NBC news 1949: door opening to reveal presenter Clifton Utley

News' rotate around the tower in the fashion of the turning of the globe or planet. This brings a sense of a news organisation broadcasting outwards from a centre point, placing itself metaphorically at the middle of the listening public. Such institution-at-the-hub-of-the-nation connotations are very different from the softer approach of the earlier NBC, where the door is pushed gently open to find a quite amicable Clifton Utley, and reveals much about the early identity of the BBC.

Figure 5.2, from 1967, suggests a shift, pointing to the immediacy of news. Here titles appear as teletype across the bottom of the screen over a still image from the lead story. The act of messages being transmitted and received is still thought to be a key part of connoting the meaning of the bulletin where the teletype can point to something up to date, reminding the viewer of the immediacy of the news and the busy communicative processes that lie behind it. Other bulletins showed hands typing rapidly on a typewriter. This represents a sense of a shift away from the authority of the news voice per se to the skills of the profession and the personalisation of the news presenter.

In the 1970s it became common to open with newsreaders preparing to speak with the news room in the background, as seen in Figure 5.3. Cooke (2005) suggests that it is important for news to appear as part of a hub of activity. These views of newsrooms are still used today, although in many cases, Peter Day of the BBC pointed out to us, they are digitally produced and dropped into backdrop screens, as on the BBC 2008 news set

(Figures 5.10 and 5.11). This means they can be shown to be busy or appearing less busy to reflect the mood of the broadcast and time of day. But in the 1970s the newsreaders appear as much more formal and upper middle class than the earlier NBC example. The choice was to character-ise television news presenters through the persona of a bank manager, a crisply groomed, middle-aged man, a little grave and very controlled.

Figure 5.2   BBC TV News, 1967: words appear as if from teletype over a zoom into a still picture

Figure 5.3   BBC newsroom, 1970: a hub of activity

Some bulletins from the later part of the 1980s, and even some contemporary bulletins, notably show presenters initially unlit in front of a lit backdrop, making them appear only as silhouettes. The lights would be raised at the beginning of the news programme and then lowered at the end, to leave again only silhouettes. This was a particularly dramatic staging device. Set designer Nik Callan, who has been working in news design for many decades and across international news outlets, spoke of the importance of lighting to create different moods for different kinds of bulletins. Raising the lights at the start of a show is a classic theatre device for dramatisation. And it signifies the shift from the phase of preparation behind the scenes into the realm of the act of news presenting itself. Before the lights go on we don't generally assume that whispers from behind the stage are part of the show. As the news ends and the lights are then lowered it is often the case that we see presenters chatting with each other in silhouette. Of course in early morning news this chatting has been drawn into the actual performance. The period of light therefore can connote a shift to formality. But this also points to the way that news needs to dramatise itself. How would we feel if our doctor or bank manager did the same when we went to see them?

It is important that in 1970 viewers were still regularly being shown the clock before the news. This can be seen across many international bulletins. Later fast digital countdowns became common in sequences to point to the precision and timing that is an intrinsic part of news. The use of the clock was unique to news bulletins and helped to signal that news was somehow momentous. Its firmly fixed time slot also brought a sense that this was a reliable and fixed entity, a fact of life, that other TV programmes and schedules worked around. The silence while the clocked ticked down adds to a sense of solemnity, gravity and above all precision. The clock here is part of the way the news communicates its grandness and authority. Even where clocks are no longer used, sound is used in the form of regular, light pulses to suggest the measurement of time or a countdown. News fuses with the rhythms of the day and of global events.

In the ITN 1984 clip (Figure 5.4) we find something new in opening sequences that now remains a common feature. A fast zoom leads in to a fixed photograph of the Earth and then aerial shots of London and the Houses of Parliament, where 'News at Ten' appears over a zoom into the clockface of Big Ben accompanied by the booming chimes of the clock. On the one hand, this is typical of how British news bulletins align themselves with powerful institutions. On the other hand, the quick

Figure 5.4   ITN, 1984: a space image of Earth

zooms into the different still images suggest that the news viewpoint is one that takes us closer to events with breathtaking speed.

Also of note in this opening sequence is the use of a real Earth that stands still. Opening sequences now commonly use globes, but these are shown in motion and are always abstracted animations and rendered as graphics. Typical of contemporary opening sequences is that they consist of several elements moving rapidly in counter directions. Often the Earth spins and rings rotate around it in different directions or pulse down the planet. At the same time other objects, which may resemble TV screens, shift past horizontally or in a much wider orbit. And, as can be seen in this image, beams of bright light burst out of the surface and fly around the planet. These might emerge from major cities and often fly into orbit. They are suggestive of breaking news flying out as beams of light.

The image of the world map was always important in news, even in the early days of Clifton Utley, and was often positioned behind the newsreader. But here, in these new sequences, the view from space and then the shifting orbits and viewpoints of the computer-generated images suggest a more commanding and versatile viewpoint. This connotation of world news can be challenged by scholarly research, which shows that news in fact is dominated by events and persons from elite countries and is sourced for the most part from a handful of Western news agencies. This has been challenged by organisations that represent non-Western countries (Machin and Niblock, 2006). A range of news studies show the extent to which this leads to an overall bias in world news that favours the interests and definitions of powerful Western nations (Cottle, 2009) rather than presenting a true global view.

Introductory sequences such as the ones described above are easy to make in modern computer software or can be purchased as templates. Figure 5.5 shows a screenshot from an AfterEffects package. A transparent globe rotates across the screen as circles of red boxes and clear white bands, also rotating, move upwards and downwards. A set of lines evoking the pattern of longitude markers on a second globe rotates moving away from the first. The whole scene is suffused in optimistic clean white light. A section of the globe carries a graph chart, which then spreads across the globe. A line of red shoots into orbit around the planet.

A number of features play important communicative roles in this example. Globes are seen from lots of different and innovative viewpoints. The Earth no longer looks real as shown through a photographic representation, but is abstracted and often transparent, suggesting something more easily graspable, honest and open. And it also makes it appear more lightweight and airy. In semiotic terms this has the meaning potential of opaque versus transparent. And we might ask how this less than real globe shifts the obligations of news coverage. Scholars

Figure 5.5 News template in AfterEffects

have argued that visually such symbolic representations have become typical of advertising and of lifestyle magazines where there is a shift to a more idealised representation of reality. In this case, however, the globe itself also becomes part of connoting high technology alongside which the news seeks to align itself.

The globes spin and move around, not only in a fixed orbit, but quickly and in exciting ways. News is shown to be about rapid movement, but not so quick that it is chaotic. The camera viewpoint is always shifting as if going on a short dynamic journey in order to eventually stabilise in an ordered fashion and in a place that becomes a vantage point, sometimes directing the gaze at the news programme's logo. The news bulletin is the stable viewpoint on all the buzzing excitement of world events.

Often the name of cities will be typed as in old teletype or somehow produce beams of light up from the planet surface as reports of news events shoot out, leaving bright trails, to be delivered at the speed of light. We see marked lines of latitude or other devices that suggest measurement and calibration, connoting objectivity along with a sense of pinpoint accuracy. The institutionalised processes of news-gathering and news-values are represented as these fast bursts of spontaneous shooting energy that come from key global cities. Scholars have noted the trend in news bulletins competing to be the bringers of breaking news, even though much of what comprises television news is prescheduled events and faux 'liveness' (Cottle, 1999). This usually involves a correspondent offering their own superficial comments on what they see in a two-way exchange with the presenter. Live news gives the impression that it is showing what is happening, as it is happening, without really showing why it is happening (Tuggle and Huffman, 2001). Cushion sees this all as not so much journalism but more akin to commentating on a sports event (2012: 80). This is news that is more about what people can immediately see rather than an agenda driven by the traditional who, what, where and why questions.

These speeding images and flashes of light point to this immediacy and 'as-it-happens' nature of the bulletin in ways that are not found in earlier introductory sequences. One problem with this use of technology is that, as Cottle (1999) points out, it can easily result in floating platitudes where analysis is sacrificed for immediate but shallow commentary on live events. Scholars have been highly critical of the way that the signposting of immediacy in news, facilitated by technology, glosses over many shortcomings in a news industry run on diminishing budgets and in desperate competition for viewers. Most news in fact does not use live images but comes from wires and is produced in the studio (Lewis and Cushion, 2009). We are told that news brings us all the breaking stories, and we see journalists in a war zone or area affected by flooding. But the need to broadcast news 24/7 means these apparently live scenes are often repeated throughout the day or allegedly 'live' fillers are used. This sense of the importance of breaking news, as opposed to reporting the details of national political events and processes, as was common in news bulletins in the past, is seen as a growing convention (Lewis and Cushion, 2009), imported in the first place from the US (Thussu, 2007).

News graphics and news sets are now more set up to connote this sense of rapidness and immediacy. With bursts of light and fast shifts in camera position, strap lines, called Astons, speed across the bottom and logos appear on the screen to help dramatise and thematise the programme. A conflict may get an image of people shouting and raising their arms, or it may be illustrated using a clip of an explosion.

Figure 5.6 shows another version of an introductory sequence, from CNN. It involves a fast journey down a number of twisting metallic tubes, then emerging into a scene of generic news images on screens, which are embedded into some kind of machine. A number of authors have pointed to CNN's pioneering role in news graphics (Cooke, 2005; Foote and Saunders, 1990). When the cable channels arrived they brought with them new types of graphic presentations. CNN was noted for the new ways it found to represent the Gulf War by showing attacks,

Figure 5.6   CNN, 2013: opening sequence

technology and maps. This had a huge influence on how the networks themselves present news. Foote and Saunders (1990) point to the use of graphics to squeeze news scenes and correspondents in over the shoulder of the anchor, with fast-moving words and images peeling off as if page by page. This opening sequence reveals a range of techniques to create movement, energy and pace.

In the CNN case, we see the headline 'Nigerian troops kill 20 suspected militants'. As this appears on the screen streams of light speed us through tunnels and digital screens spin and shift, with other generic news images of explosions and extreme weather. But the Nigerian case is not the same as weather. And it has a complex social and political context founded in colonial history, which is missing from the report itself. Missing too are any kind of details about the actual demands of the 'militants' and in whose interests these troops act. But this report is fused with the meanings carried by the semiotic choices of movement, speed, immediacy, colour, technology, liveness, etc. The question we need to ask is not so much whether this is dumbing down but what actual discourses are carried by the visual elements.

News sets and projected images

We also spoke with Peter Day and with news set designer Nik Callan about the importance of news sets. These too carry important meanings, ideas, attitudes and values about news. We saw this above in the difference between the 1940s NBC set, with its wooden chair, and the later ITN studio using a news team working away busily in the background to provide context for its news readers. Just before this time it was common to see lone male presenters sitting behind a counter in front of a curtain, a map of the world or a clock. Callan said that these were typical of the old style of presentation, which lacked the depth and light now expected by news audiences and also help to create a greater sense of drama.

The older sets stem from the times of the news reader as bank manager or as formal family doctor and as authoritative. But this has changed. Contemporary news sets fall into one of two categories, although Callan said that most use a combination of the two: the virtual and the real set. The look of the virtual set has been a huge influence on the look of physical sets. These virtual or semi-virtual sets are cheap and flexible to set up in almost any space once the software is purchased and installed. And they can be easily tailored to make the news slightly different for different news slots and audiences. The BBC has used different colours throughout the day, with pink in the morning and then darker blues throughout the day. And different colours have been used to brand for different global feeds. All this can be done with the click of a mouse.

In his article 'The Future of Television Graphics' (2008) Edsall discusses the massive change brought about by the move away from physical sets for the presentation of television programmes to sets that involve growing numbers of digital components. News programmes have definitely embraced this change. Figure 5.8 illustrates the use of a virtual set for the BBC news, something the BBC themselves are keen to talk about (http://www.youtube.com/watch?v=vQ26-v8Nzo0 [the video is no longer available]), although not necessarily in terms of the semiotics of the design choices. Figure 5.7 shows how the simple set, even in 1993, can be transformed into something that glows with high key lighting and space age command centre looks.

This shift to virtual sets has been facilitated by new technologies. Older chroma-key technology was the technique of replacing one colour with a video source. The classic example is the weather reader who was seen in front of a weather map. One problem with this technique was that sharp edges were usually seen around the person standing in front of the graphics. And if the key was not set up exactly this sharp edge could even form a slight halo around the presenter. Nevertheless viewers became schooled in ignoring such details. Another problem was the need for a flat screen to project against.

Figure 5.7   BBC news: raw set

But the development of virtual sets through the Ultimate keying system in the 1990s allowed much more seamless merging of images and actual physical objects, of foregrounds and backgrounds. One important part of this technology is the process of 'ray tracing', which uses specialist software to analyse the way that light particles are likely to move around a scene. The software is able to map the geography of the setting on to which a digital image is to be overlaid. Realistic shadows can thereby be inserted into virtual scenes. A flat screen was no longer required. Such a system is costly to install. But once this is done many different shows can be shot from the studio simply by loading a different program. Callan said that many of the sets he designed were developed to be multi-purpose, and especially to be used for different bulletins throughout the day.

More recently cheap software combines a number of camera angle possibilities and easy management of the insertion of personalised elements such as video footage and news images behind presenters, etc. One of the main manufacturers of the technology is Accom.Inc who created a package called ElsetLive, which gives more realistic textures, depth and perspectives. The real advantage of this for the designer, according to Edsall, who is a designer himself, is that in these sets the laws of the real world can be ignored. So walls and objects can be transparent, float in space or be animated in more spectacular ways. The BBC (Figure 5.8) used a huge cut glass crest hanging in the air in front of the desk.

Figure 5.8   BBC news: set with virtual element

We often find news programmes using composite sets. These contain some real elements, which are then fused with virtual elements. One simple use for this can be to make very small news studios appear much larger. Or as in the BBC's case it can be used to add outside scenes or virtual production centres behind the real set. On the Breakfast News the presenters sit in front of a view out over London at sunrise on a glorious day. This can be replaced by views of the newsroom or images of news stories, as we see in Figure 5.10. Callan spoke of the way that the shift to High Definition (HD) causes problems with this process as it reveals more details in the backgrounds more clearly. Formerly a painted scene would look sufficiently real, but in HD it is immediately apparent that it is merely a painting. This is a problem because, as Callan explained, a painted backdrop of London, for example, would often combine landmarks that could never be seen in one shot together in a real-life photograph, to facilitate the viewer seeing and recognising 'London' from any camera angle.

Figure 5.9 shows a TV news set from Singapore, which serves as a good example of how a cityscape in the background can add depth as well as locate a set in a given geographic location, in this case Singapore.

Figure 5.9   Singapore news set

In the two shots of the 2008 BBC news studio (Figures 5.10 and 5.11) we can see the way that the virtual elements can be modified for shows at different times. Callan spoke of the need for comfort and brighter, soft lighting for the morning news to create a wake-up feel, and darker effects with more angular lighting for the later bulletin. This combination can increase a sense of formality and gravity as it draws out lines and angles. In Figure 5.11 we also see the use of the background computer-generated news room with huge images of terrorist suspects positioned in the foreground.

In the case of local TV news a softer set with a more relaxed atmosphere may be appropriate. Presenters' chairs will appear more comfortable, moving away from the authoritative black leather office chair of national news studios. The audience is meant to feel closer to the news presenters and the environment they are shown in, which is important in helping them identify with the programme as being local and familiar to them, making them feel part of the news. Whereas national news studios need to create a sense of distance, a sense of important global news happening far from the viewer's home and being broadcast from a location far from their everyday experience.

Callan also pointed to several other key features of contemporary news set designs that can be seen in Figures 5.10 and 5.11. One is the creation of depth, which he said was important in creating drama. And the BBC evening set can be seen to use a particularly large amount of space. In fact, as Callan pointed out, this sense of space can be generated through

Figure 5.10   BBC: morning news set

Figure 5.11 BBC: evening news set

Figure 5.12 ZDF Heute Journal: set design

the virtual part of the set. In Figure 5.12 the set from the German ZDF Heute Journal features the theme of the globes, but here the virtual backdrop creates a huge sense of space. Opening scenes favour presenters as appearing quite minute against large images.

We saw the role of space as an associational metaphor when considering the design of modern newspapers. The association of the ability to physically move in space can be transferred to page composition to give a sense of 'liteness', of accessibility and of airiness. This too is important in the case of news sets. Ample space communicates a sense of luxury, power and magnitude. It also generates a different sense of the identity of the newsreader. As we see above, the part-virtual set appears large with oceans of empty space. In a former time we might have found it covered with typewriters and files. But now news studios feel like the cathedrals of the news landscape: expansive with lots of empty space. Communication is now clean, fast, smooth and uncluttered.

In the Heute Journal case we find the globes loom above the set, again suggesting international coverage. But these also work to bring a sense of magnitude and something interstellar, with all its connotations of journey, wonder, advanced technology and epic human activity. For Ekström (2000), this is a shift away from the journalism of information to the journalism of attractions, where viewers are wowed by speed and spectacle.

On these huge sets it is common to find presenters, acting as specialists, able to walk around in a business-like way in front of the huge screens and often to interact with them. Much more will be said on this when we look in detail at a specific news package in the next section.

Callan, too, pointed to the importance of colour. Colour can be designed in the set or can be added virtually to allow easy manipulation. This could be used to signal up different markets. On the BBC set in Figure 5.11 a wider colour palette can be used to indicate a more lively morning mood. But it can also be used to create depth by putting bars of colour in the background. Colour can also be used to make elements rhyme to give a designed feel to news, as we found in the use of colour on more modern versions of newspapers. Interviews with newspaper designers revealed that younger readers were no longer attracted to the more sombre and authoritative model of news. While this does not necessarily signal a shift to tabloid styles, as we saw in Chapter 3, it does change standards and visual qualities. Just as with the new free newspapers that use colour, fonts and space to set themselves apart from more traditional publications with an 'informer' role, TV news uses colours that hint at a different, more modern viewing experience.

The identity of journalists and news in a television news report

So far we have looked at how the identity of journalists, news organisations and what they do and stand for are communicated through opening sequences and sets. These tell viewers what news is and who journalists and news organisations are. Such visuals provide the meaning of the news stories that follow in the manner that newspaper designs help provide the meaning and attitude of the news they carry. This sense of defining who journalists are, why we should trust them, and what the meaning of news is continues into the bulletins themselves. So we now shift our attention to how this happens visually within news packages themselves. Alongside the actual content, viewers are continually given cues as to why and how journalists have authority and the kinds of relationship we have with them.

A number of scholars have shown how even subtle cues in language, posture and gesture by news anchors and reporters are key in the staging of news and their expertise to do so (Montgomery, 2007; Ekström and Kroon Lundell, 2011). At a simple level Moore (2009) points to the role of the news anchor in claiming to align with and represent the feelings of the nation. Writing on CBS Evening News anchorman Walter Cronkite, he notes Cronkite would look embarrassed when the news embarrasses the nation, shocked when the news shocks the nation and laugh when the news is amusing. And in fact since that time there has been considerable debate as to whether this strategy of presenting the news is useful as it conjures a sense of accessibility by delivering a sense of familiarity to homes of viewers. Or whether famous, over-familiar news readers, along with other celebrity reporters, are in fact damaging to the journalistic community as a whole (Meltzer, 2010). The visual presentation of the news items can similarly have an evaluative role of news as the voice of the nation.

News readers have generally been shown sitting behind desks, although this is changing. And they do so while sitting up straight but slightly inclined forwards, with elbows and hands resting gently on the table in front of them. This in itself is a very different convention than we found back in the 1940s, when Clifton Utley sat and leaned slightly back away from the viewer, with arms folded. In this case there was a sense of slight informality and certainly of a little disengagement from the viewer. We can imagine the difference between being in a meeting with a colleague who sits back in this way, less engaged, compared to one who sits forward and more upright, leaning slightly in towards other colleagues. In the latter case there is a greater sense both of alertness, but also of increase in personal proximity. However, in the case of news anchors this is only slight. On the other hand, if an anchor was to lean much further forward, such intimacy would seem inappropriate. So even at the level of posture we are being given cues about the attitude of the journalism that is being presented.

Ekström and Kroon Lundell (2010, 2011) looked at the subtleties of the way the anchor indicates through gesture and tone of voice that the correspondent who will now provide the details of the report just introduced is authoritative and expert. Kroon Lundell and Ekström (2013) have also delivered a range of important observations on how the way journalists present themselves as experts has changed greatly since the 1990s, leading to a shift away from the reporter as witness on site to one where they themselves have increasingly been used as experts, brought into the studio. Journalism is said to have become increasingly interpretative in the way news is presented (Neveu, 2002; Djerf-Pierre and Weibull, 2008). Cushion (2012) suggests that more and more junior journalists are having to give comments on a massive range of topics that they know little about. Kroon Lundell and Ekström (2013) argue that we now inhabit an era where we find reporters increasingly appearing as cocky expert interpreter, who, in a rather arrogant manner, questions the comments and actions of others. And importantly, they note, this is often done with a slight nod and wink in the direction of the public (2013: 529).

This switch has gone along with a transformation in the way that stories are presented by correspondents as experts in the studio. Kroon Lundell and Ekström (2013), comparing interactions between anchors and expert reporters on set, say that interaction is now almost stylishly sociable – what Montgomery describes as slightly gossipy in character. The anchor themselves switches to the role of 'inquiring mind' (Ekström and Kroon Lundell, 2011). For the most part scripted exchanges between news presenter and correspondent are staged as the former, in a concerned and respectful manner and with furrowed brow, presents the latter with the chance to demonstrate their expertise.

Another feature of the visual presentation of news bulletins as discussed by scholars is the need to signify liveness. News items must retain a sense of spontaneity and be firmly based in the here and now, even where they clearly are not. Couldry (2004) points to liveness as one way that news legitimises its claim to be a central institution for representing social reality. Bourdon (2000) suggests that liveness is linked to journalism's professional ideological values, such as authenticity and truth, along with spontaneity, all of which are associated with the breaking news story as opposed to the planned and scripted report. Kroon Lundell (2009: 272) says that liveness therefore is something that has to be 'recreated or re-enacted in order to hold the audience's attention'. Ellis (2000: 33) argues therefore that news, although pre-recorded and highly scripted, will use devices such as direct address, direct gaze and eye contact, collective personal pronouns such as 'us' and 'we', which bring about a sense of intimacy and immediacy, and use phrases like '... reports' and 'soon to come'.

Huxford (2007) has also commented that liveness can in some instances mean little more than the use of devices for indicating visual proximity and creating an 'eye-witness' feel. Visual symbols such as police emergency tape in the background may be included in the frame for that purpose. Journalists may be seen dressed in military fatigues or yellow windbreakers, which also suggest their proximity. Zelizer (1990) has written that journalists must align themselves in some way with the setting that has been communicated. This can be achieved metonymically, such as where a 'for sale' sign on a lawn can represent rising house prices or a supermarket can in the same way represent inflation (p. 667). She suggests that these scenarios create the illusion of liveness, where at the end of the report the journalists will sign off, restating their location, even if in between much of what has been shown is not actually live at all.

The idea of bearing witness, along with TV's basic need to have footage, has brought about another kind of shift in the content used in news programmes. News outlets themselves have had fewer staff and less resources to produce their own footage, and so have had to look to commercially exploit their own assets to generate revenue. Big news providers such as CNN and ABC are now able to exploit their massive archives of news reports and raw footage, which can then be used as visual filler for news packages. Machin and Jaworski (2006) examine the way that archive clips are used in a number of news packages. They look specifically at the ITN archive, which had over 600,000 hours of news film footage and offices in London, New York, Los Angeles, Johannesburg, Tokyo and Paris. ITN states that its footage is accessed around the world:

> Many of the world's prominent producers, broadcasters, corporations, new media ventures and film makers have used the ITN Archive to find exactly the right footage, shot or clip for their project.

Here the word 'project' glosses over the way that the use of pre-prepared footage interferes with the ideology of spontaneity and bearing witness. The ITN archive allows news editors to search among categories such as 'crime' or 'war'. Within these categories they can search for 'terrorists' or 'crime scenes' with details of camera angles and what is seen. Machin and Jaworski (2006) look at the use of archive clips in several stories. One story on the Middle East peace process is visualised by stock footage of masked gunmen. A story on possible strikes by public service workers uses footage of skirmishes between police and the public, although it is not clear who these people are or where, along with a single shot containing the Houses of Parliament – and in fact no strike had yet taken place. For news editors these sorts of shot help to visualise stories where footage is a problem. Events are realised through generic ideas. Palestinians are not conveyed as actual people with real issues but generic thugs and gunmen. Employees concerned about cuts in public services are represented as anonymous figures skirmishing with riot police.

One further shift in television news has been the introduction of graphics software that can provide simple lists of bullet points or be completely immersive. In our interviews news producers spoke of the use of Vizrt software that can be used for everything from basic graphics such as maps and the insertion of images and quotes into the screen to immersive graphics that appear to fill the studio set, as often seen used in national elections.

While some scholars have sought to carry out empirical tests as to whether such graphics aid remembering or comprehension of stories (Fox et al., 2004), others have been more critical in questioning the extent to which such visual theatrics can replace actual detailed analysis. As mentioned before, Ekström (2000) argues that these create a news television of 'attractions'. He is clear that he is not suggesting that news should not entertain, and sees the division between information and entertainment as a misleading one. But he says we can think about the intentions of news producers, whether to inform, tell stories or to attract. There is a continuum from a point where the desire is to inform, through one where the rhetorical strategies of storytelling are used to create drama, to one where spectacular strategies are used to attract, shock and fascinate viewers (p468). And these three parts of the spectrum aim at different kinds of viewer involvement, from detachment, to involvement in dramatised and personalised events, which can involve empathy, to the lust to gaze where we see something spectacular, visually highly stimulating or the forbidden (p468). Importantly for our concerns in this chapter, the journalist shifts from an informer to a storyteller, then finally to arranger or exhibitor. In the news of information the focus is on transparency of sources and the nature of information. In the television news heavy on swirling graphics the news switches to the need to capture and hold attention. In interviews with staff at BBC World News we heard about the constant struggle to hold on to BBC values of impartiality while at the same time thinking about how to retain the attention of the viewers, who are known to rarely make it even halfway through a whole bulletin.

Individual authors such as Carruthers (2011) have also been highly critical of the way that graphics can bring a sense of explanation but can replace an actual analysis. She gives the example of news reports of war, which can take the form of elaborate interactive graphics of manoeuvres, with explosions and military hardware that can conceal an absence of contextual and political analysis. Machin (2007), looking at news info-graphics, shows how scenes of wars are clearly ideologically shaped to take attention away from issues of politics and aims, and even of destruction and effects on civilians, to emphasise equipment, technology and troop manoeuvres.

We now look at an example of a single specific news package to see how presentation and footage are shaped to provide cues as to why and to what extent news now creates a sense of the authoritative.

BBC News, August 29, 2012: Nick Clegg calls for a temporary tax rise for the wealthy in society

We examine an example of the visualisation of a press release by BBC news with a view to looking at how journalism, journalists and news are represented. This is a press release by the British Liberal Democrat party in 2012, saying that the Deputy Prime Minister, Nick Clegg, was calling for a tax rise for the wealthy in a time of austerity. This press release, as it was covered across the news media, appeared to contain no strategic details of how this was to be implemented or who exactly would be considered as 'the wealthy'. The release, made as part of the annual party conference, can be seen as part of an attempt to distance the party from the harsher austerity policies of the Conservative Party with whom the Lib Dems had formed a coalition government. This news coverage of politics, anchored around PR and events and announcements, made and packaged specifically for journalists, as opposed to actual analysis of policies, is, a number of scholars have observed, characteristic of broader patterns of political reporting (Franklin, 2004). And there has also been criticism (Deacon, 2004) that journalists are now out of touch with the way political power is distributed and operates in British society since men of the newer organisations, semi-private bodies or quasi-government, are simply off their radar. This particular report is characteristic of these patterns. We see the sequence of clips, along with the scripted dialogue in Figure 5.13.

This story will have been chosen on the planning desk the evening before, from what, as BBC news producer Alice Salfield told us, would be for the most part other press releases. The day's news producer and the

Figure 5.13 BBC news bulletin, visual sequence

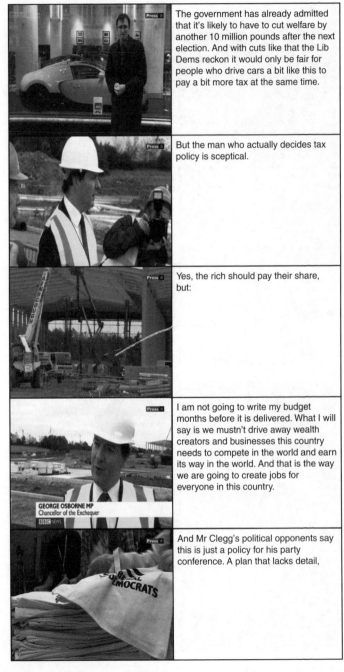

Figure 5.13 (Continued)

	designed simply to boost his flagging support among voters and Lib Dems.
	What he's doing is chasing headlines. Trying to placate very angry Lib Dem supporters and former voters at a time when they are absolutely exasperated with the fact that he is doing in government totally the opposite of what he's now saying. **CHRIS LESLIE MP** Shadow Treasury Minister BBC NEWS
	So a new debate over tax has begun. A call from Nick Clegg that the poor should not face more austerity alone. But there is no detail
	over how much more cash he wants Britain's rich to hand over. James Landale, BBC News Westminster.

Figure 5.13 (Continued)

so-called 'newsorg' would then distribute tasks and look into the logistics of sending out film crews and reporters. For each story the planning desk will work out what is needed in terms of, Alice told us, balance of viewpoints, visual interest and requisition of archive footage or graphics. There is no story boarding, as it would take up too much time, but a sense of the segments that are needed to make the package. A larger number of stories then will be shared out with producers and reporters assigned a number each, although many will not come to anything. Individual reporters, she said, would also come up with their own ways to make a story more visual during filming, perhaps by carrying out interviews with the public.

This particular story begins with the news presenter introducing the story, providing a summary of the stances provided in three interviews they had generated for the package, from a Lib Dem MP, the Chancellor of the Exchequer and the Shadow minister.

The role of the news anchor in establishing the visual tone and attitude of a news programme has been discussed earlier on in this chapter, but it is worthy of note that the anchor in this case looks squarely into the camera. Kress and Van Leeuwen (1996) would account for this as a 'demand image', where the viewer is encouraged to have a relationship with them. Their style of dress is also notable. It is not so much formal and authoritative, as it is power dressing with a touch of glamour. The dress colour is black, giving the impression of elegant evening wear. As Kroon Lundell and Ekström (2013) report, there are often now connotations of the stylishly social in the look and manner of news readers, in contrast to the older-style bank manager and family doctor look.

The anchor reads the summary points of the story and then frowns and lowers her voice slightly as she passes us over to the political editor who provides the actual report. As Ekström and Kroon Lundell (2010, 2011) have noted, these are typical features by which the expertise and authority of the reporter-as-expert are signalled for the viewer. We are also later told that the political editor reports from Westminster. There is in fact no clear sense that any of the material comes from Westminster itself, or even that it would need to. But this is part of signalling up liveness and being on the spot. News bulletins often show journalists outside of courtrooms or police stations where events may have happened previously or 'where police are interviewing suspects as we speak', all in the name of signifying spontaneity and of an immediate view of a social reality that news requires for its self-legitimisation. This is what Huxford (2007) describes as simulated proximity (p. 661).

From the view of the anchor, sitting in front of the BBC's deconstructed globe that we see in the opening sequences and the digitally generated news room seen behind it, we cut to a graphic of money falling over a map of the UK, which is itself covered in money. This is repeated throughout the package. Alice told us that such graphics would typically be considered where no interviews or archive footage were feasible or available. Julien Cousins of BBC World News told us that some stories such as politics and business don't lend themselves to exciting visuals, so there is a need to be creative. This graphic is the first of a number of attempts to make the story more visually dynamic. But what is the effect of these graphics and to what extent do they help the story? Is this a journalism of information? In fact this graphic symbolises the UK and the taxation system without providing any background information. The comments made by Clegg and those of the other politicians who challenge him float free of any kind of context. We are never told what the current state of tax payments is.

We also find a section that uses stock aerial footage of large houses. It is of note here that the footage is aligned with the season when the package was produced. Alice told us that when using archive footage it would always be important to match this to the weather in other footage used. It would not do, for example, to have bleak rainy archive footage used during a heat wave or vice versa. Again this is about connoting immediacy. Linking is not done through the tightness of relevance and information need, but through the need for visual continuity.

So in this news package the current situation as regards taxation of richer and poorer people is not explained at all but rather is symbolised by falling money and the 'wealthy' are symbolised by large houses. Britain is a country where it is known that the largest proportion of tax is paid by poorer people and where corporations can pay no tax at all while making billions of pounds of profit each year (Guardian, 2013). Oxfam has released a report about the vast increases in wealth inequalities in the world as a whole, mentioning the trillions held in tax havens (Hobbs, 2013). And the UK was responsible for one-in-five global tax havens, more than any other country (Anderson, 2013). These are also times when bankers are being bailed out for their excesses by public money while those at the bottom suffer cuts in pay, benefits and services (Irvin et al., 2013). And there are groups of accountants and economists publicising alternative, clearly formulated, policies for dealing with debt that involve investment in public services and corporate tax rather than austerity. But these tended to fall off the news radar and also violated news values of simplicity and a need for showing elite people holding positions of power.

We could reasonably argue that this kind of news report helps to inhibit greater public understanding and also that it is largely failing to interrogate the assumptions of neoliberalism. Salfield told us that for such a story there would be a need to gain a balance of perspectives for the requirements of impartiality and also to fulfil broader news conventions. The visual strategy used here to gain this impartiality is the fact that three representatives of different views are interviewed. Yet nothing in the rest of the visual treatment provides the differentiated backdrop that could communicate the complexities mentioned above. The visuals simplify and gloss over the starker realities behind this news story.

We also find the classic on-the-spot report where the journalist walks towards the camera while gesticulating with his hands. Scholars have noted one increasing trend in television news involving a switch away from investigation and reporting to on-the-spot witnessing (Montgomery, 2007). Cushion and Lewis (2010) have been highly critical of news that shows correspondents delivering reports from locations but with very little actual explanation or context.

Salfield told us that BBC reporters often had to be creative in order to bring visual interest to a story. But an important part of the report is also that the journalist indicates who they are, their level of authority and their relationship to the viewer. While the reporter wears sombre formal clothing, suggesting a serious mission of bringing events to the viewer and his place among the powerful in Westminster, his manner is personal. We saw above that scholars describe how the reporter becomes the authority and expert, and interprets rather than presents. And he gesticulates and frowns while walking towards the camera as if trying to work it all out on the spot when it is in fact scripted. There are other notable moments that underline the personal nature of the report. He refers to 'us' as the people, in contrast to the wealthy. There is something conspiratorial in his attitude to the viewer, with a slightly dismissive over-the-shoulder thumb gesture towards the cars that are used to indicate wealthy people in the sequence. And he also deals with and presents the sound bites from the three politicians in a slightly wry manner. This is just the kind of cocky and arrogant manner Kroon Lundell and Ekström (2013) suggest now increasingly characterise the modern reporter. And the car showroom from where the journalist reports is the classic metonymical use of visuals providing the sense of place and proximity to issues to give it the desired eye-witness feel.

Other visual filler material comes in the form of the building site scene where the Chancellor of the Exchequer speaks and later with several scenes from the Lib Dem party conference. The building site scene also appears to greatly favour the way the Conservative minister is represented as part of constructivity and progress. Here he states that it is businesses that will take the country forward and provide everyone with jobs. The neoliberal agenda is not questioned, and crucially nor is the assumption that in a post-industrial society and global economy full employment could never again be achievable, which he presents as unproblematic. None of these statements are interrogated by the reporter. But there are clear reasons for this.

Scholars have given much attention to the way journalists use interviews with sources, and especially with politicians. One key theme in research is these 'sound-bites' or 'image-bites' such as used in the above news package. Some researchers have found a pattern of decreased length of these bites, and in turn an increase in time given to journalists framing and interpreting these (Farnsworth and Lichter, 2007). Blumler and Gurevitch (2001) see this as a fragmentised and interventionist style of journalism. And importantly, how the fragments are used and what the viewer sees are more determined by the needs of the journalists to create narrative relevance than by the actual contents of the replies of those who are interviewed (Nylund, 2003). Ekström and Kroon Lundell (2010) have shown how reporters seek out sound bites that fit with narrative requirements, so that stories can then be assembled based on what has been made available and what is usable. Most importantly, perhaps, as Eriksson and Östman (2013) point out, the adversarial stance that these kinds of political interviews take is little more than strategic ritual. It is about enacting the watchdog role of news.

In this news package, the actual issue of taxation and policies is never actually dealt with in an adversarial manner. But since there is a 'balance' of political viewpoints from the mainstream political parties that are forged into a simple narrative, the watchdog role can be signified.

Conclusion

Journalism is in the unique position of being able to shape the public image of its own activities. We have seen that this has clearly changed over time. Journalism presents itself as fast and furious, highly techno-logical and not so much global as 'interstellar'. At the same time there has been a shift away from an alignment with traditional authority and of informing, as we saw with the press, to a more informal position where reporters are now able to provide wry and often quite arrogant interpretations of events and personalities while at the same time claiming to speak as one of us with a nod and a wink. While introductory sequences connote the fast journey of news stories and exciting viewpoints, in the end these may increasingly be the smug and fairly uninformed opinions of non-specialist journalists while producers and editors have to work harder to find signifiers of 'liveness' and 'on-the-spot' reporting as resources dwindle.

Conclusion

The process of researching this book has been fascinating, not least because new developments in the world of visual journalism seemed to be happening at a breath-taking speed even as we were writing. Tablet devices hadn't been invented when we set out. Then suddenly magazine and newspaper apps were a distinct part of the visual journalism landscape.

This process of acceleration of technological advances in the production of news has been ongoing for some time, and part of the reason why we wanted to write this book was to chart the huge impact this has had on the way news looks, is packaged and delivered to its audiences. From the outside looking in it is easy to get the impression that it's all change, that journalism is at the very forefront of the brave new digital world. But after many hours spent talking to people working in the field of designing and packaging news messages of all kinds, our general sense is that traditional working processes are still very much alive and that it is the basic principles of visual design that still underpin the way visual journalists work. These may be amended and adjusted, of course, to accommodate new platforms and new digital production processes, but in many ways these are not so different from what they were 30 years ago. One of the biggest changes we found was the more sophisticated and widespread use of the fundamentals of design, new, more considered ways of using images and composition, and more focus on specific markets. All these cut across platforms.

Applying theoretical models such as multimodal analysis to our investigation of visual journalism has highlighted that there are identifiable patterns that underlie visual communication across all print and digital media. It would seem that they are mostly subconsciously applied by practitioners, but are also universally and correctly received and understood by viewers in a large part of the globe, certainly in the Western world. No matter what form any new medium takes or what gadget it is viewed on, those general rules of what certain fonts, colours, densities, weights, spacing, sizing and combinations thereof imply stay the same.

Our research showed that it is partly the availability of certain new features within web and tablet design that have given designers the ability to be as precise as they'd like to be with font-styling and spacing, for example. In the past they may have liked to be, but were hampered by technical limitations. But the audience's desire for things to look great grows with the ability of designers to fulfil that desire. One practitioner told us about how even a lag of a fraction of a second while swiping from one page to the next in an iPad app had become very much noticeable and very much unacceptable to viewers. Expectations about what news media visuals should deliver are growing. And this project has made us reflect on the extent to which the nature of what journalists do, of the products they produce, may have been misrepresented by too much emphasis on content in a text-and-information sense. What we mean here is akin to the idea of the medium being the message. What readers and viewers get through visual journalism is an experience alongside which they can align, which speaks to them on a range of levels. To reduce this to matters of information and citizenship on the basis of written content may be misleading, although it is also easy to see why scholars and theorists have prioritised language for analysis, over other modes of communication.

A common complaint of practitioners, in the US and Europe, was the problem of shrinking budgets. The funds for all kinds of news-gathering and production processes are diminishing. But there is a perceived, although often not well understood, need to invest in the technical development and maintenance of digital platforms that live up to audiences' expectations. This includes not least of all the need to take on new IT-confident staff. But journalism studies tend to take a critical approach to the demise of the older, larger news organisations rather than a desire to understand the new kind of freelance and entrepreneurial environment. Often journalism training institutions were slow to give up an older model of journalism and reporting to embrace the new kind of media environment where the older skills could still have an important place.

We have also found that, while designers are obviously focused on creating aesthetically pleasing layouts for online platforms and TV, there seemed to be a growing trend towards the generic. This seems to be partly caused by financial restrictions. Online libraries for stock photography are so successful, because they offer the cash-strapped editor the opportunity to buy high-quality images at bargain prices, amounts that undercut even the most humble photographer's day rate. But our research in Chapter 1 shows that a photographer who works for a stock library has to produce shots that will be malleable enough to work in the context of various different outlets, whereas a photographer hired and briefed by one publication can produce something far more idiosyncratic and original, specifically suited to just that one publication in look and style. It could be argued that that photographer can be more creative and does not need to rely on cliché quite as much. But photographers, no matter what position they worked in, were still mindful of markets and what elements and styles a 'quality' image should carry. Images for a photo essay should have visual depth and have a stylised sense of colour, for example. That doesn't mean to say that images such as Tom Stoddart's work on women living in a war zone can't give the viewer painful insights into daily lives. But the photojournalists themselves are keenly sensitive to news cycles, news hooks and where their work can sell.

The trend towards the generic is exacerbated in visual journalism by the fact that digital technology makes design more easily and quickly replicable. With larger numbers of practitioners having to engage in the visual side of news delivery, those that are less familiar with the processes and the tools involved will logically rely upon default templates, set ups, graphs, fonts and style choices that are pre-programmed. Ready-made website masks are available, just waiting to be populated through a content management system. At the time of writing magazine templates were selling in their thousands with the prospective editor simply having to choose between available 'interior design', 'business' or 'extreme sports' themes, among others, to fit their requirements. Once articles were slotted into the pre-designed pages, they were ready to publish. This to some extent is the fast food equivalent for news visuals. On the one hand, we might see these positively as allowing what are, at the point of origin, quality designs to be made by experienced professionals. Even in-house corporate and public institutional magazines come to have a more professional look. But, on the other hand, we come to inhabit a design landscape that becomes limited in its language.

Both authors give regular talks in universities around the world, and have noticed that at most of them more or less identical in-house magazines can be found everywhere. Such publications take elements of corporate style to point to open space, 'room to think', but also to 'fun', 'accessibility', 'innovation' and social relevance, all of them important concepts in times of the increasing commercialisation of education. But we ask what happens when templates that present set selections of design elements and features – even to connote 'the creative', 'the edgy' and 'the innovative' – become common in the world's visual language.

Across interviews with top designers we found that the way photographs and visual design elements are used has changed in some respects, while still being underpinned by key traditional skills. And new generations of readers and viewers are being schooled to not notice these changes.

These certainly are interesting times for the world of journalism. Online news and digital platforms have become a fact of life. During the early stages of researching this book there still seemed to be some debate as to whether it was a good idea for newspapers and magazines to have gone online. The process of media diversification seemed to be beginning to change towards a process of media migration as print versions of some newspapers and magazines began to cease publication and to become available online-only. Doom-sayers felt the end of print journalism looming. But as we're nearing completion of the book a more multi-facetted and subtler view of the potential futures for news visuals is emerging.

While it seems nigh on impossible to predict just what type of gadgets will be the news vehicle of choice tomorrow, from Google glasses to holographic projections, everything seems within the realms of the imaginable, most people we spoke to seemed positive and optimistic about the possibilities that current developments were creating. Some seemed unsure whether iPad apps were going to be the news medium of the future or whether they would ever be adopted in great numbers. Most seemed to agree that print journalism was far from dead, however. They thought that as different methods of delivering news information to audiences developed, they would start to fulfil distinct and different functions, each medium becoming increasingly good at fitting its particular niche. Digital platforms seemed to be more likely to be set to become the provider of fast-paced, quick, picture-led news, while print media would potentially settle into a role of delivering longer, more considered, more in-depth pieces, providing the long-form background information to the constant flow of quick and dispensable news bites. It seems plausible that the visual style of print and digital news might specialise more and more to suit those two different functions. Giving any more precise predictions as to where visual journalism is heading would be little more than conjecture.

One aim of this book was to bring together theory and practice in visual journalism. We believe that in many ways we have achieved this, and that it has been a helpful and unique approach to use. Designers, as we found throughout the interviews we carried out for the book, tend to not talk about what they do in systematic terms. Many will list the sequence of stages that redesigns involve, such as consulting with a range of parties. They will talk about market needs influencing the look of a particular webpage or television set design. But the details of decisions such as the nature of a typeface, the use of a colour, or the choice of a particular element in a news set are normally accounted for in terms of them suiting the brand, them providing authority, restraint or energy.

Throughout the book we show that there are basic principles underlying the building blocks of design. Of course, it is the talented and experienced designer who is able to use these building blocks well, but what we have indicated is that clear patterns can be identified and be used as entry points for analysis. Understanding these patterns can also help with building our own designs. But, importantly it is the information provided by the visual journalists that allows us to understand design as a practical and deliberate communicative activity carried out in specific contexts for specific reasons. Newspapers and websites get design awards for creativity. But this tends to foster the idea that the visual is a mere decoration, a container. We have shown throughout this book that this is simply not the case. Designers work alongside advertisers, marketing professionals and also journalists to target products and to address people in different ways. Readers recognise themselves and their information and entertainment needs in a newspaper, a website or a news set. It is this specific information provided by the visual journalists that allows us to understand the goings on that lie behind the visual design building blocks that we have identified and analysed.

In the Introduction we also mentioned the importance of reflective practice. One thing we have not done in this book is include the way journalists reflected on our own analyses. And in fact while the visual journalists we interviewed were interested in the kinds of questions we were asking of their work, and the analytical tools we were using, we found it difficult to have dialogue. One of the authors has been giving talks at design conferences, and it is clear that there is a growing interest in theories of design and visual communication within the profession. But, unlike in mainstream journalism studies, this theory is itself rather new. The most productive meeting of minds in this sense was with the photojournalists. They tended to be more aware of criticisms of the image and associations with truth claims. And the ways they saw their own work, as meeting the needs of typical news flows, news priorities and news genres, was very much aligned with the kinds of concerns raised in the academic literature. This was particularly rewarding from our point of view as it made us rethink the nature of these kinds of criticisms and the degree to which they understood what photojournalists think as they take their photographs. Scholars take a set of standards from the very elite part of the profession and then refer to these as a point of analysis across what is a vastly broad and diverse industry. Much theorisation about journalism itself is done in the context of a lofty sense of the role of journalism in citizenship and democracy, whereas most successful journalists operate as professional writers in massively different contexts.

What also became more and more apparent to us as we carried out interviews for the book was the international nature of visual journalism. One the one hand, many of our visual journalists work around the world, designing newspapers, television sets and websites. Or they work for syndication agencies that sell their work around the world. This was certainly the case as regards photojournalism and magazine, newspaper and web template design. On the other hand, visual journalists look outwards to international designs. Successful professionals know the best work being done in different countries and which designs receive awards. We found that in countries that have emerging commercial media industries, such as in China and Vietnam, visual journalists look outwards for their inspirations and models. Again here there is place for more research to document these patterns. Scholars have done wonderful work on the nature of elite journalism in terms of reporting around the world, but visual journalism and how it sits alongside this has received little attention.

We hope our book offers opportunity for reflecting on what visual communication is and how its role could be defined. All of the visual journalists we interviewed spoke of their work as not simply being about the look of a magazine, a website or television news bulletin but as their designs being part of the product's meaning, as their work being a fundamental part of what the journalistic message conveyed will mean to the reader and viewer. In the Introduction we suggested that it is not so much that we live in a more visual society but that how we communicate has changed. This includes both language and visual communication, but also involves a process where the role formerly occupied by language has been taken over by design, or at the very least design is gradually beginning to take on a parallel function to language. We have wonderful examples of this throughout this book as websites, magazines and news sets have been transformed as part of telling readers and viewers about the contents and about what the experience is of engaging with the media. A magazine design can allow a reader to experience its contents as authoritative, but yet a part of a thinking community; a television broadcast can tell viewers that news is high-tech and immediate; a tablet design can tell a user that they are using the latest technology, spreading this meaning to the cutting-edge nature of the design.

Of course, this research pointed out the way that readers and viewers have changed. Not only have their visual expectations of design changed, but how they assess and relate to information has changed. They are now trained not only to grasp this new kind of multimodal communication but have been led to have the expectation that media address them correctly through it. It should be tailored in terms of content and appearance for is proper context, with degrees of 'seriousness', 'informing', 'accessibility', 'warmth' and other kinds of emotions.

These readers and viewers have also changed their views of what is an authoritative kind of information. We saw across the chapters that news audiences no longer tolerate the former 'news as authoritative voice'-type product. Journalism can claim to have an information value, but this must be presented in light of the way the niche market sees itself, as a critical thinker, as someone who is socially and design aware. As our visual journalists pointed out, such people may have little social awareness or style awareness beyond having a consumer sense of style. But the design must acknowledge such self-perceptions. A news magazine can rebrand itself to foreground its role as an information provider, but it is nevertheless required to do so through the appropriate kinds of compositional features that also signpost independent thought and analysis – a kind of level of expertise in the reader generally not considered by traditional kinds of news outlets.

In many ways these kinds of findings should not be surprising. So the media landscape now allows more choice in one sense, meaning that it becomes more important for these media to signal up how they address such choices. And visual journalism as a whole, over the past two decades, has played an important part in shifting much of the world's visual landscape. In another sense behind these choices often lie more limited sets of actual real possibilities. Social media such as Facebook, at the time of writing, were heralded as an individual or small community kind of media. Yet millions of users were operating within the same templates. In terms of visual journalism we may live in a world of proliferation and creativity. But, given this is driven by commercial concerns, that is, those of advertisers, to what extent will this mean increasingly operating within globally shared templates clustered around ideas and attitudes related to specific marketing categories? Certainly these are exciting questions that call for more research, and the answer may well be a little of both.

References

Allen, S. (2006) *Online News: Journalism and The Internet*. Maidenhead: Open University Press

Andén-Papadopoulos, K. and Pantti, M. (Eds) (2011) *Amateur Images and Global News*. Bristol: Intellect Books

Anderson, B. (1991) *Imagined Communities*. London: Verso

Anderson, S. (2013) Poor Nations Deprived of Billions as Half of Investment is Channelled through Tax Havens. *The Independent*, Thursday 23 May

Baines, D. and Kennedy, C. (2010) An Education for Independence: Should Entrepreneurial Skills be an Essential Part of the Journalist's Toolbox? *Journalism Practice*, 4(1), 2010 (online)

Barnett, S., Seymour, E. and Gaber, I. (2000) *From Callaghan to Kosovo: Changing Trends in British Television News 1975–2000*. London, University of Westminster

Barthes, R. (1978) *Image, Music, Text*. London: Fontana

Becker, K. (1992) Photojournalism and the tabloid press. In: P. Dahlgren and C. Sparks (Eds), *Journalism and Popular Culture*. London: Sage

Bennett, L. (2005) *News – the Politics of Illusion*. London: Longman

Berger, P. (1980) *Ways of Seeing*. London: Penguin

Bird, E. (2010) Introduction: The Anthropology of News and Journalism: Why Now? In: *The Anthropology of News and Journalism: Global Perspectives*. Bloomington, IN: Indiana University Press

Blumler, J.G. and Gurevitch, M. (2001) Americanization Reconsidered: UK/US Campaign Communication Comparisons Across Time. In: Lance Bennett and Robert Entman (Eds), *Mediated Politics: Communication in the Future of Democracy*. New York: Cambridge

Boczowski, P.J. (2009) Materiality and Mimicry in the Journalism Field. In: B. Zelizer (Ed.), *The Changing Faces of Journalism: Tabloidization, Technology and Truthiness*. London and New York: Routledge, pp. 56–67

Bolza, H. (1967) Friedrich Koenig und die Erfindung der Druckmaschine. *Technikgeschichte*, 34(1): 79–89

Bourdon, J. (2000) Live Television is Still Alive: On Television as an Unfulfilled Promise. *Media, Culture & Society*, 22(5): 531–56

Bouvier, G. (2014) British Press Photographs and the Misrepresentation of the 2011 'Uprising' in Libya: A Content Analysis. In: D. Machin (Ed.), *Visual Communication*. Berlin: De Gruyter, pp. 281–300

Boyd-Barrett, O. (2000) National and International News Agencies: Issues of Crisis and Realignment. *Gazette*, 62(1): 5–18

Briggs, M. (2009) *Television, Audiences and Everyday Life.* Buckingham: Open University Press

Carruthers, L. (2011) *The Media at War,* 2nd edn. London: Palgrave Macmillan

Chalaby, J. (1996) Journalism as an Anglo-American Invention: A Comparison of the Development of French and Anglo-American Journalism, 1830s–1920s. *European Journal of Communication,* 1/3: 303–26

Chen, A. and Machin, D. (2013) Changing Genres and Language Styles in Contemporary Chinese Lifestyle Magazines. Media International Australia, *Incorporating Culture & Policy* 147: 73–84

Chen, A. and Machin, D. (2014) The Local and the Global in the Visual Design of a Chinese Women's Lifestyle Magazine: A Multimodal Critical Discourse Approach, *Visual Communication* 13: 287–301

Compton, J.R. and Benedetti, P. (2010) Labour, New Media and the Institutional Restructuring of Journalism. *Journalism Studies,* 11(4): 487–99

Conboy, M. (2006) *Tabloid Britain: Constructing A Community through Language.* London: Routledge

Conboy, M. (2014) Visual Aspects of British Tabloid Newspapers: 'Image Crowding Out Rational Analysis'?, in Machin, D. (ed.) *Visual Communication.* Berlin: De Gruyter, 261–280

Conboy, M. and Steel, J. (2010) From 'We' to 'Me': The Changing Construction of Popular Tabloid Journalism. *Journalism Studies,* 11(4): 500–11

Cooke, L. (2005) A Visual Convergence of Print, Television, and the Internet: Charting 40 Years of Design Change in News Presentation. *New Media and Society,* 7/1: 22–46

Cottle, S. (1999) From BBC Newsroom to BBC News Centre: On Changing Technology and Journalistic Practice. *Convergence,* 5/3: 22–43

Cottle, S. (2009) *Global Crisis Reporting.* Maidenhead: Open University Press

Couldry, N. (2004) Liveness, 'Reality', and the Mediated Habitus from Television to the Mobile Phone. *Communication Review,* 7: 353–61

Cousins, C. (2012a) How Web Design Has Changed Print. http://tympanus.net/codrops/2012/06/13/how-web-design-has-changed-print/

Cousins, C. (2012b) Perfectly Paired: Using Symmetry in Web Design. http://tympanus.net/codrops/2012/09/04/perfectly-paired-using-symmetry-in-web-design/

Cousins, C. (2012c) Understanding the Rule of Thirds in Web Design. http://tympanus.net/codrops/2012/05/23/understanding-the-rule-of-thirds-in-web-design/

Crosbie, V. (2004) What Newspapers and their Web Sites Must Do to Survive. *USC Annenberg Online Journalism Review,* 4 March. www.ojr.org/ojr/business/1078349998.php

Crozier, M. (2010) A Golden Age of Design and Journalistic Excellence in the UK after the Wapping Strike of 1986: The Rise of New Technology and the Death of the Print Unions with special reference to *The Independent* 1986–1993. PhD Thesis, City University

Cushion, S. (2012) *Television Journalism*. London: Sage

Cushion, S. and Lewis, J. (Eds) (2010) *The Rise of 24 Hour Television News: Global Perspectives*. New York: Peter Lang

Deacon, D. (2004) Journalists and Quasi-government in the UK: Conflict, Co-operation or Co-option? *Journalism Studies*, 5: 339–52

De Beer, A. S. and Merrill, J. C. (eds) (2004) *Global Journalism. Topical Issues and Media Systems*. Boston: Pearson

Djerf-Pierre, Monika and Weibull, Lennart (2008) From Public Educator to Interpreting Ombudsman: Regimes of Political Journalism in Swedish Public Service Broadcasting 1925–2005. In: J. Strömbäck, T. Aalberg, T. and M. Ørsten (Eds), *Political Communication in the Nordic Countries*. Göteborg: Nordicom, pp. 195–214

Edge, S. (2008) Urbanization: Discourse Class Gender in Mid Victorian Commercial Photography: Reading the Archive of Arthur J. Munby (1828–1910). *Critical Discourse Studies*, 5(4), November: 303–17

Edsall, S. (2008) The Future of Television Graphics. *ACM SIGGRAPH Computer Graphics*, 42(2) [online]

Ekström, M. (2000) Information, Story-telling and Attractions: TV-journalism in Three Modes of Communication. *Media, Culture and Society*, 22: 465–92

Ekström, Mats and Kroon Lundell, Åsa (2010) Beyond 'the Broadcast Interview': Specialized Forms of Interviewing in the Making of Television News. *Journalism Studies*, 12(2): 172–87

Ekström, Mats and Kroon Lundell, Åsa (2011) The Joint Construction of a Journalistic Expert Identity in Studio Interactions between Journalists on TV News. *Text & Talk*, 31(6): 661–81

Ellis, J. (2000) *Seeing Things: Television in the Age of Uncertainty*. London: I.B. Tauris

Eriksson, G. and Östman, J. (2013) Cooperative or Adversarial? Journalists' Enactment of the Watchdog Function in Political News Production. *The International Journal of Press/Politics*, 18/3: 304–24

Farnsworth, S.J. and Lichter, S.R. (2007) *The Nightly News Nightmare: Television's Coverage of US Presidential Elections, 1988–2004*. Lanham, MD: Rowman & Littlefield

Flusser, V. (1984) *Towards a Philosophy of Photography*. Göttingen: European Photography

Foote, J. and Saunders, A. (1990) Graphic Form in Network Television News. *Journalism Quarterly*, 67(3): 501–07

Fox, J.R., Lang, A., Chung, Y., Lee, S., Schwartz, N. and Potter, D. (2004) Picture This: Effects of Graphics on the Processing of Television News. *Journal of Broadcasting & Electronic Media*, 22(3): 646–74

Franklin, B. (1997) *Newszak and News Media*. London: Arnold

Franklin, B. (2004) *Packaging Politics*. London: Bloomsbury

Franklin, B. (2006) *Local Journalism and Local Media: Making the Local News*. London: Routledge

Franklin, B. (2010) Introduction to special edition on The Future of Journalism. *Journalism Studies*, 11/4: 442–63

Freedberg, D. (1989) *The Power of Images: Studies in the History and Theory of Response*. Chicago: University of Chicago Press

Freund, G. (1980) *Photography and Society*. London: Gordon Fraser

García Avilés, J.A., León, B. and Sanders, K. (2004) Journalists at Digital Television Newsrooms in Britain and Spain: Workflow and Multi-skilling in a Competitive Environment. *Journalism Studies*, 5(1): 87–100

García, E.P. (2008) Print and Online Newsrooms in Argentinean Media: Autonomy and Professional Identity. In: C.A. Paterson and D. Domingo (Eds), *Making Online News: The Ethnography of New Media Production*. New York: Peter Lang, pp. 61–75

Garcia, M. (2002) *Pure Design*. Nijmegen: Miller Media

Garfield, S. (2011) *Just My Type: A Book About Fonts*. London: Profile Books

Gillmor, D. (2011) The Rise of Citizen Photojournalism. *Mediactive*, 15, March http://www.aljazeera.com/indepth/opinion/2011/03/2011314134026456445.html

Goldman, R. and Beeker, G.L (1985) Decoding Newsphotos: An Analysis of Embedded Ideological Values. *Humanity & Society*, 9, August: 351–63

Griffin, M. (2004) Picturing America's 'War on Terrorism' in Afghanistan and Iraq: Photographic Motifs as News Frames. *Journalism*, 5(4): 381–402

Guskin, E. (2013) Newspaper Newsrooms Suffer Large Staffing Decreases. http://www.pewresearch.org/fact-tank/2013/06/25/newspaper-newsrooms-suffer-large-staffing-decreases/, 25 June

Halkasch, H.-J. (1993) *Biografisches Lexikon des Druck- und Verlagswesens: Lebensdaten und Leistungen*. Itzehoe: Verlag Beruf und Schule

Halliday, M.A.K (1978) *Language as a Social Semiotic: The Social Interpretation of Language and Meaning*. Oxford: Oxford University Press

Hansen, A. and Machin, D. (2008) Visually Branding the Environment: Climate Change as a Marketing Opportunity. *Discourse Studies*, 10/6: 777–94

Hartley, J. (1996) *Popular Reality: Journalism, Modernity, Popular Culture*. London: Arnold

Hayes, J. (2010) Facts and Figures: Television Programs in China. http://factsanddetails.com, April

Herbert , J. (2001) *Practicing Global Journalism. Exploring Reporting Issues Worldwide*. Oxford: Focal Press

Hobbs, J. (2013) The Cost of Inequality: How Wealth and Income Extremes Hurt Us All. Executive Director, Oxfam International. http://www.oxfam.org/sites/www.oxfam.org/files/cost-of-inequality-oxfam-mb180113.pdf

Hodge, R. and Kress, G. (1988) *Social Semiotics*. London: Polity Press

Holmes, T. (2012) *Magazine Journalism*. London: Sage

Huffington Post (2013) BBC Journalists to Strike and Work to Rule over Easter. http://www.huffingtonpost.co.uk/2013/03/27/bbc-journalists-to-strike_n_2964550.html

Huxford J. (2004) Surveillance, Witnessing and Spectatorship: The News and the 'War of Images'. *Proceedings of the Media Ecology Association*, vol. 5

Huxford, J. (2007) The Proximity Paradox: Live Reporting, Virtual Proximity and the Concept of Place in News. *Journalism*, 8/6: 657–74

Irvin, G., Bryn, D., Murphy, R., Reed, H. and Ruane, S. (2013) *In Place of Cuts: Tax Reform to Build a Fairer Society*. London: Compass

Jameson, F. (1991) *Postmodernism, or the Cultural Logic of Late Capitalism*. London: Verso

Kahan, B. (1999) *Ottmar Mergenthaler: The Man and His Machine: A Biographical Appreciation of the Inventor on His Centennial*. New Castle, DE: Oak Knoll Press

Kanter, J. (2012) ITN to Axe 15 Jobs on ITV London News. http://www.broadcastnow.co.uk/news/indies/itn-to-axe-15-jobs-on-itv-london-news/5044028. article, 4 July

Karlsson, M. and Strömbäck, J. (2010) Freezing the Flow of Online News: Exploring Approaches to the Study of the Liquidity of Online News. *Journalism Studies*, 11/1: 2–19

Keller, J. (2011) Photojournalism in the Age of New Media. *The Atlantic*, 4 April. http://www.theatlantic.com/technology/archive/2011/04/photojournalism-in-the-age-of-new-media/73083/

Kress, G. (2010) *Multimodality*. London: Routledge

Kress, G. and Van Leeuwen, T. (1996) *Reading Images: The Grammar of Visual Design*. London: Routledge

Kress, G. and Van Leeuwen, T. (2001) *Multimodal Discourse*. London: Arnold

Kress, G. and Van Leeuwen, T. (2006) *Reading Images: The Grammar of Visual Design* (2 edn). London, Routledge

Kroon Lundell, Åsa (2009) The Design and Scripting of 'Unscripted' Talk: Liveness versus Control in a TV Broadcast Interview. *Media, Culture & Society*, 31(2): 271–88

Kroon Lundell, Åsa (2010) Dialogues between Journalists on the News: The Intraprofessional 'Interview' as a Communicative Genre. *Media, Culture & Society*, 32(3): 1–22

Kroon Lundell, Åsa (2012) Talking Politics in Broadcast Media: Cross-cultural Perspectives on Political Interviewing, Journalism and Accountability. *Journalism Practice*, 7(3): 381–82 (review)

Kroon Lundell, Åsa and Ekström, Mats (2010) Interview Bites in Television News Production and Presentation. *Journalism Practice*, 4(4): 476–91

Kroon Lundell, Åsa and Ekström, Mats (2013) Interpreting the News: Swedish Correspondents as Expert Sources 1982–2012. *Journalism Practice*, 7(4) [online]

Lackshmi, R. (2007) The Long Reach of India's TV News: Local Stories Reign in Booming Market. *The Washington Post*, 12 September

Langton, L. (2009) *Photojournalism and Today's News: Creating Visual Reality*. Chichester: Wiley-Blackwell

Levinson, D. (1983) Book Review, *The Evening Stars: The Rise of the Network News Anchors*, by Barbara Matusow, *Library Journal*, 108(14), 1469

Lewis, J. and Cushion, S. (2009) The Thirst to be First: An Analysis of Breaking News Stories and their Impact on the Quality of 24 Hour News Coverage in the UK. *Journalism Studies*, 6/4: 461–77

Lowrey, W. and Anderson, W. (2005) The Journalist behind the Curtain: Participatory Functions on the Internet and their Impact on Perceptions of the Work of Journalism. *Journal of Computer-Mediated Communication*, 10(3), Article 13

Lupton, D. (2010) *Thinking with Type*. New York: Princeton Architectural Press.

Lutz, C.A. and Collins, J.L. (1993) *Reading 'National Geographic'*. Chicago: University of Chicago Press

Machin, D. (2007) *Introduction to Multimodal Analysis*. London: Arnold

Machin, D. and Jaworski, A. (2006) The Use of Film Archive Footage to Symbolise News Events. *Visual Communication*, 5/3: 345–66

Machin, D. and Niblock, S. (2006) *News Production: Theory and Practice*. London: Routledge

Machin, D. and Van Leeuwen, D. (2007) *Global Media Discourse*. London: Routledge

Mackay, H. and Ivey, D. (2004) *Modern Media in the Home: An Ethnographic Study*. Rome: John Libbey Publishing

Macmillan, G. (2013) Telegraph to Cut 80 Jobs and Create 50 New Digital Posts in Restructure. *The Wall: Social, Marketing, Media*. http://wallblog. co.uk/2013/03/12/telegraph-to-cut-80-jobs-and-create-50-new-digital-posts-in-restructure/

Matsa, K. (2013) News Magazines Hit by Big Drop in Ad Pages. http://www. pewresearch.org/fact-tank/2013/07/15/news-magazines-hit-by-big-drop-in-ad-pages/, 15 July

McChesney, R.W. (2004) *The Problem with the Media: U.S. Communication Politics in the 21st Century*. New York: Monthly Review Press

McManus, J. (1994) *Market-Driven Journalism: Let the Citizen Be Aware*. London: Sage

Meggs, Philip B. (1998) *A History of Graphic Design*. New York: John Wiley & Sons, Inc.

Meltzer, K. (2010) *TV News Anchors and Journalistic Tradition*. New York: Peter Lang

Montgomery, M. (2007) *The Discourse of Broadcast News: A Linguistic Approach*. London: Routledge

Moore, F. (2009) America Loses Its Anchor. *Chicago Daily Herald*, 18 July, p. L2

Moore, C. (2011) Britain Shouldn't feel Guilty About the Part We Played in Ousting Colonel Muammar Gaddafi. *The Telegraph*, 26 August, http://www. telegraph.co.uk/news/worldnews/africaandindianocean/libya/8724942/ Britain-shouldnt-feel-guilty-about-the-part-we-played-in-ousting-Colonel-Muammar-Gaddafi.html

Morley, D. (1992) *Television, Audiences, and Cultural Studies*. London: Routledge

Mortensen, M. (2011) When Citizen Photojournalism Sets the News Agenda: Neda Agha Soltan as a Web 2.0 Icon of Post-election Unrest in Iran. *Global Media and Communication*, 7/1, 4–16

Neveu, E. (2002) Four Generations of Political Journalism. In: Raymond Kuhn and Erik Neveu (Eds), *Political Journalism: New Challenges, New Perspectives*. London: Routledge, pp. 22–44

Newton, J.H. (1998) The Burden of Visual Truth: The Role of Photojournalism in Mediating Reality, *Visual Communication Quarterly*, 5/4, 4–9

Newton, J. (2000) *The Burden of Visual Truth: The Role of Photojournalism in Mediating Reality*. London: Routledge

Niblock, S. (2012) Envisioning Journalism Practice as Research. *Journalism Practice*, 6(4): 497–512

Niblock, S. and Machin, D. (2007) News Production in a Digital Newsroom: Inside Independent Radio News. *Journalism*, 8/2: 184–204

Nylund, M. (2003) Asking Questions, Making Sound-bites: Research Reports, Interviews and Television News Stories. *Discourse Studies*, 5(4): 517–33

Ofcom (2010) Halt in Decline of Flagship TV News Programmes. London: Ofcom. media.ofcom. org.uk, 30 June

Pantti, M. and Wahl-Jorgensen, K. (2007) On the Political Possibilities of Therapy News: Social Responsibility and the Limits of Objectivity in Disaster Coverage, *Studies in Communication*, 1: 3–25

Pantti, M. and Wahl-Jorgensen, K. (2011) Not an Act of God: Anger and Citizenship in Press Coverage of British Man-made Disasters. *Media, Culture & Society*, 33(1): 105–22

Parry, K.J. (2010) A Visual Framing Analysis of British Press Photography during the 2006 Israel–Lebanon Conflict. *Media, War and Conflict*, 3.1: 67–85

Patterson, T.E. (2000) *Doing Well and Doing Good: How Soft News and Critical Journalism Are Shrinking the News Audience and Weakening Democracy – and What News Outlets Can Do About It*. John F. Kennedy School of Government, Harvard University

Pavlik, John V. (2000) The Impact of Technology on Journalism. *Journalism Studies*, 1(2): 229–237

Peer, L. and Ksiazek, T.B. (2011) YouTube and the Challenge to Journalism: New Standards for News Videos Online. *Journalism Studies*, 12(1): 45–63

Peters, C. (2011) Journalism To Go: The Changing Spaces of News Consumption. *Journalism Studies*, 13(5–6): 695–705

Pew Research (2010) How News Happens: A Study of the News Ecosystem of One American City, Project for Excellence in Journalism. http://www.journalism. org/analysis_report/how_news_happens, 11 January

Press Gazette (2011) Digital Editions Account for Less Than 1% of Mag Sales. http://www.pressgazette.co.uk/node/47731, August

Project For Excellence in Journalism (2011) The State of the News Media, Pew Research Center, http://stateofthemedia.org/2011/overview-2/

Reason, R. (2013) http://ronreason.com/designwithreason/2013/11/20/magazine-redesign-exploring-display-type-during-prototype/

Rosler, M. (1989) In, Around, and Afterthoughts (on Documentary Photography). http://education.victoriavesna.com/sites/default/files/pdfs/Rosler-In_around.pdf

Silverstone, R. (2006) *Media and Morality: On the Rise of the Mediapolis*. London: Polity

Sjovaag, H. (2011) Amateur Images and Journalistic Authority. In: K. Andén-Papadopoulos K. and M. Pantti (Eds), *Amateur Images and Global News*. Bristol: Intellect Books, pp. 79–98

Sontag, S. (1973) *On Photography*, London: Allen Lane

Sontag, S. (2004) *Regarding the Pain of Others*. London: Picador

Sweney, M. (2013) Trinity Mirror to Cut More Than 90 Regional Roles in Digital Content Move. *The Guardian*. Available at: http://www.guardian.co.uk/media/2013/jan/29/trinity-mirror-digital-content, 29 January [Accessed 10 April 2013]

Syal, R., Bowers, S. and Wintour, P. (2013) Big Four Accountants Use Knowledge of Treasury to Help Rich Avoid Tax. *The Guardian*, Friday 26 April

Taft, R. (1938) *Photography and the American Scene: A Social History, 1839–1889*. New York: Dover

Tagg, J. (1988) *The Burden of Representation: Essays on Photographies and Histories*. London: Macmillan

Temple, M. (2006) Dumbing Down is Good For You. *British Politics*, 1/2: 257–73

Thussu, D.K. (2007) *News as Entertainment: The Rise of Global Infotainment*. London: Sage

Tuggle, C.A. and Huffman, S. (2001) Live Reporting in Local News: Breaking News or Black Holes? *Journal of Broadcasting & Electronic Media*, 45/2: 335–44

Tunstall, J. (1996) *Newspaper Power*. Oxford: Oxford University Press

Turner, V. (1982) *From Ritual to Theatre*. New York: PAJ Publications

Ursell G. (2003) Creating Value and Valuing Creation in Contemporary UK Television: Or 'Dumbing Down' the Workforce. *Journalism Studies*, 4(1): 31–46

Van Leeuwen, T. (2005) *Introducing Social Semiotics*. London: Routledge

Wahl-Jorgensen, K. (2009) On the Newsroom-centricity of Journalism Ethnography. In: S.E. Bird (Ed.), *Journalism and Anthropology*. Bloomington, In: Indiana University Press, pp. 21–35

Wayne, M., Petley, J., Murray, C. and Henderson, L. (2010) *Television News, Politics and Young People: Generation Disconnected?* London: Palgrave

Weber, J. (2005) Straßburg 1605: Die Geburt der Zeitung. *Jahrbuch für Kommunikationsgeschichte*, 7: 3–27

Wring, D. and Ward, S. (2010) The Media and the 2010 Campaign: The Television Election? *Parliamentary Affairs*, 63(4): 802–17

Zelizer, B. (1990) Where is the Author in American TV News? On the Construction and Presentation of Proximity, Authorship and Journalistic Authority. *Semiotica*, 80: 37–48

Index